FROM FEMALE SEMINARY TO COMPREHENSIVE UNIVERSITY:

A 150-Year History
of Beaver College
and Arcadia University

Edited by

Samuel M. Cameron

Mark P. Curchack

Michael L. Berger

Photo Research by

Samuel M. Cameron

Arcadia University

Glenside, Pennsylvania

Arcadia University and the editors have made all attempts to insure that the events and people described in this book were portrayed faithfully. However, as the sources included occasionally conflicting archival materials, as well as the recollections of individuals, there may be inaccuracies.

Arcadia University and the editors have also made all attempts to identify the persons portrayed in photographs, and to attribute those images to the photographers who made them. In several instances it was impossible to determine who is pictured or the source of the photograph. We regret failures to identify both subjects and photographers, and invite the reader to identify either so that we may update our records.

The book was designed by art270, Inc. of Jenkintown, Pennsylvania, and edited by Samuel M. Cameron, Mark P. Curchack and Michael L. Berger.

The main text of the book was set in Adobe Goudy. The essays were set in Adobe Helvetica Light. Alice Lawler, Marie T. Gallagher and Reid J. Smith proofread the book. Image scanning by art270, Inc., Baker Printing & Graphics of Beaver, Pennsylvania, and Innovation Printing of Philadelphia, Pennsylvania. The book was printed using 200 line screen separations by Innovation Printing, on 110 pound White Reflections Dull text. The binding is by Hoster Bindery, Inc. of Ivyland, Pennsylvania. This book was printed in an edition of three thousand copies.

Arcadia University
450 South Easton Road
Glenside, Pennsylvania 19038-3295
Phone: 215-572-2900
www.arcadia.edu

Library of Congress Control Number: 2002112982
ISBN 0-9725352-0-9

FOREWORD

I have always considered it a privilege and my special good fortune to be the President of this fine institution. To serve in that role at the time of the 150th anniversary is a particular thrill. I often look back on the more than thirty years I have been part of the Beaver College and Arcadia University community, and marvel at the changes I have seen. Now, we have this wonderful book to show us how far we have come and the rich and responsible educational legacy that has brought us here. As you will see, it has been a remarkable journey that has prepared us for a limitless future.

When the idea of a commemorative volume was first proposed to me, I had no idea of the historical treasures that would be discovered, and surely no conception of the pictures that would be assembled. Through the words and images of this book, you will experience our history from our founding before the Civil War in a small town on the Ohio River through our early years as a university. Changes in curriculum, changes in rules, and certainly changes in fashions will unfold before you, while certain core values and traditions endure. You will see scenes of the special places in Jenkintown and of the beautiful Harrison estate in Glenside, perhaps views of people you remember. You will learn of the often extraordinary devotion, and sacrifice, that enabled us to survive in the hardest times and the creative energy that continues to allow us to lead the way in educational innovation.

Many people must be thanked for making this project come to life. The acknowledgements section details the many friends on this campus and in Beaver, Pennsylvania, without whose assistance so much could not have been done. I wish to note with thanks the numerous alumni who responded to calls for recollections and memorabilia.

Most of all, though, I offer my personal appreciation and praise to the editorial team that actually created this book. I do not know how Mike Berger, Vice President for Academic Affairs and Provost, and Mark Curchack, Dean of Graduate and Professional Studies, found the time to do all the work that has gone into this volume. Their deep and abiding loyalty to the institution comes through in their effort. The heart and soul of this project, however, reflects the stellar performance of Professor Sam Cameron. Sam was the driving force behind the book, much as he has long been a bedrock of the Psychology Department and the faculty at large. His dogged pursuit of photographs, historic documents, and memorabilia has been extraordinary, yielding surprise after surprise. Our understanding of our past has grown exponentially, nearly all on the basis of what Sam discovered. Sam actually retired from the faculty mid-way into this work, but true to his nature, he forged ahead with even greater gusto. I have the feeling we will see more discoveries by him even after this book is printed.

I hope that all who read this volume share in the fascination I feel as I turn the pages, and take great satisfaction in seeing a personal reflection in the story that unfolds. We know that every college and university is the sum of the experiences of its students, faculty, staff, alumni, trustees, and friends; this is especially true of Arcadia University. Enjoy this rich narrative, and add it to the memories in your heart.

Bette E. Landman

Bette E. Landman
President

INTRODUCTION

A copper dragon that stood guard on the roof of the now demolished conservatory that once graced the patio of Grey Towers Castle. Several identical dragons can still be seen guarding the patio on the south side of the building. (Photo by Jerome Lukowicz, Philadelphia, Pa.; Arcadia University Archives)

Institutions, much like people, use the occasion of large, round-numbered anniversaries to do something special. When he saw that Beaver College/Arcadia University was approaching its 150th year, Vice President for Academic Affairs Michael Berger suggested to the President that a history of the institution might be written for the event. The idea was greeted enthusiastically, and the search began for a possible author. At about the same time, Dr. Samuel Cameron, a Professor of Psychology, was granted a sabbatical to write a series of articles regarding the College's early years in Beaver County. His research there revealed a treasure trove of information concerning the institution's history. This happy confluence of events led to the creation of this book's editorial committee—Dr. Cameron, Dr. Berger (who has background as an historian), and Dr. Mark Curchack, Dean of Graduate and Professional Studies (and the author of two institutional self studies).

No one imagined what bounty we would encounter. And no one expected that a professor of psychology would turn into a highly proficient historical sleuth. During Dr. Cameron's sabbatical year, he made frequent trips to Beaver County and to Harrisburg to search for documents and pictures. His painstaking reading of Board minutes, records of the Methodist Church in Pittsburgh, newspapers, and letters, revealed details about key turning points in our past that had either long been forgotten or had been misunderstood, sometimes for decades. In addition, he uncovered an incredible collection of old photographs, mined the often-disorganized University Archives, and interviewed alumni who lived through some of the notable events of our past.

This volume is the result of that labor, of contemporary research undertaken by our colleagues and ourselves, and of the work on our history that has gone before. It contains five main sections, plus a bevy of additional essays. The first three sections derive, nearly in total, from the only "published" work on the College's history, *Beaver College—the First Hundred Years*, printed in 1954 to celebrate the Centennial, written by Ruth L. Higgins, Dean of the College and Professor of History and Government, and Mary S. Sturgeon, Assistant Professor of English. These sections cover, respectively: 1) from the founding of the institution in 1853 to the end of the term of President Taylor, one of the most influential figures in our history;

2) from that point in 1894 to the 1924 crisis which led to the move east to Jenkintown; and, 3) from the establishment of the Jenkintown campus to the time of the 1953 Centennial Celebration. We have tried to remain true to the language and style used by Professors Higgins and Sturgeon, inserting explanatory statements, in brackets or in footnotes, when needed, but we deleted some sections of the original text containing details unnecessary for the current project—hence, the ellipses throughout the first three chapters. The fourth section covers the story of the institution from the consolidation on the Glenside campus to its emergence as Arcadia University. It too has its origins in original source material—an essay by Dr. Margaret F. LeClair, Dean of Graduate Studies. This was a history of the College to 1980, incorporating much of the Higgins and Sturgeon material. It has been modified and updated concerning happenings since 1980. The final section contains a vision for the future, authored by the person whose vision has guided us for more than twenty years, President Bette Landman.

Some of the essays accompanying the core historical narrative highlight particular episodes in the story of the institution, such as the decision to leave the Pittsburgh area. Some essays describe special occurrences (such as the campus visit of Rudyard Kipling) or important features of the institution (Grey Towers Castle). Still others detail key parts of the institution, such as Graduate Studies and the Center for Education Abroad.

And then there are the pictures, so many pictures of people, places, events, so many surprises. All of these—whether unearthed on glass slides from museums in Beaver County, or retrieved from the various university archives—have been lovingly assembled by Dr. Cameron.

In the space of this volume, we cannot hope to do complete justice to all the people who made a difference in the history of Beaver College and Arcadia University. This has long been an intensely collegial institution, and thus we feel even more keenly the failure to name each individual who has been involved in our success. Similarly, we have needed to make choices about which events and deeds to include or overlook. Even a small institution can have an amazing degree of complexity, making it impossible to chronicle all that it does. We are confident that all those who played roles in this history will be gratified to see the institution evolve in this narration, and take personal satisfaction in that story whether or not they are individually identified.

You are about to read an account of an institution beloved by thousands of alumni and friends. You will see that our 150 years of life was not a certain thing; that several times we have come close to the brink of dissolving. Thanks to the loyalty, generosity, and commitment of people at key moments—from a few leaders or benefactors to the entire faculty—we have pulled through and, at last, pulled ahead. This volume appears at an unprecedented time in our history, with greater enrollment, greater capacity, and more self-sufficiency than at any time in the past. It is likely that new crises will occur, but we are sure that we will overcome them, to carry on the spirit of learning and growth that has always been at the core of our mission.

We invite you to enjoy this journey of a century and a half, and to take pride in the role you may have played in bringing that about.

ACKNOWLEDGEMENTS

In the middle of the 20th century, a plain gold key was awarded upon completion of one year of service on the Student Council. The President of the Council received a gold key with the College seal set in onyx, such as the one pictured here that was awarded to Barbara Goodwin '49. (Photo by Jerome Lukowicz, Philadelphia, Pa.; Arcadia University Archives)

The major pictorial and historical discoveries for this book resulted from a serendipitous meeting in France between Samuel Cameron and Frank and Carin Batchelor of Beaver, Pennsylvania. All were on a University of Pennsylvania Alumni tour of Burgundy, France, and happened to have dinner together the first evening. During the ensuing conversation, it turned out that Mr. Batchelor knew more of the College's early history than Dr. Cameron did. Mr. Batchelor and his wife invited the Camerons to be their guests later that fall so that they might together learn more about the early days of the College in Beaver, Pennsylvania. The Camerons were to be guests of the Batchelors two more times during the research on this book, hospitality that greatly facilitated Dr. Cameron's research on the early history of the institution.

During those visits Mr. Batchelor introduced Dr. Cameron to many of the leading citizens of the town, all of whom were helpful and enthusiastic in support of the research project. One was Norman S. Faulk, a retired lawyer and avid historian of the town and county of Beaver. It was he who, over lunch, suggested that Dr. Cameron might look at some uncataloged glass lantern slides in the basement of the Beaver Area Historical Museum. His suggestion led to the discovery of 83 photographs from the earliest days of the College. Robert A. Smith, Director of the Beaver Area Heritage Foundation and Chairman and Director of the Beaver Area Historical Museum, went through the slides with Dr. Cameron, had them professionally scanned, and generously arranged the Museum's permission to use them in this book. The majority of the images that illustrate the first third of this volume are reproduced with the kind permission of the Beaver Area Historical Museum.

Others in Beaver, Pennsylvania, who helped uncover vital information included: Dr. Betty Sue Schoughnessy, Superintendent of Beaver Area School District, who made available documents relating to the School District's purchase of the Beaver College property in 1925; Mr. James Carver, member of the Board of Trustees of Beaver Cemetery, who arranged access to the records of the cemetery; Rev. Ralph P. Cotton, Pastor of the Beaver United Methodist Church, who provided a history of the Church; Barbara Gordon '59 and her husband F. Wallace Gordon, publisher of the *Beaver County Times*, who provided the photograph of the demolition of College Hall; and Midge Seften, Archivist for the Beaver

Area Museum, whose ability to locate items in the Museum's archives at a moment's notice proved to be invaluable.

Other archivists and research librarians who lent assistance in this project were: Mr. William Waybright, Archivist of the Western Pennsylvania Conference of the United Methodist Church; Dr. Dale Patterson, Archivist of the General Commission on Archives and History of the United Methodist Church; David R. Ginnell, Archivist at the Historical Society of Western Pennsylvania, Heinz Pittsburgh Regional History Center; Kenneth Ross, Research Librarian of the Presbyterian Historical Society; C. W. Evans, Research Librarian of the Rare Book Collection, Library of Congress; and Kevin Walsh, Philadelphia Orphans' Court Records. Most important and helpful of all has been Ann Ranieri, Head of Technical Services in the Landman Library at Arcadia University, who has been a source of constant support.

This volume uses many photographs and images. Where the photographer is known, credit is given. Unfortunately, we often were unable to determine the names of many of the photographers whose images are used. While we cannot recognize them individually, we would like to acknowledge their professional contribution.

A number of alumnae also have contributed to this history. Phyllis J. Weiner '51 and Elizabeth Felton Fox '49 provided pictures and information about Dr. Jack Wallace's 1948 summer program in Europe. Alice Mazurie '73 donated the "On Strike" Beaver College t-shirt. Rosemary Deniken Blankley '57, Barbara Heylman Longstreth '58, and Betty Holton Weiss '60 provided information on the institution's athletic history. Kathryn E. Darby '44 read the essay "Traditions of the Past" for accuracy. Many others have sent in memorabilia and information that helped form the background for this history.

We would like to express particular gratitude to the entire Arcadia University academic community. The understanding and cooperation of our colleagues allowed this project to move forward against the day-to-day demands of institutional life. We give special thanks to President Bette E. Landman. Her enthusiasm and generous support were a constant inspiration and help during the writing of this book. She also provided the lead that resulted in the discovery of the Kipling dessert plates in the Library of Congress. Her friendship with Dr. Lorna Dupheney Edmundsen, President of Wilson College, turned up the picture of Dr. William Curran.

We also would like to thank Arcadia staff members Bill Avington, Dottie Ettinger, Marie Gallagher '95, Stacy Kelly, Nancy Magid, Phyllis McNeff, Hal Stewart, Tarajean Trzaskawka '98, Donna Whitlock, and Lorraine Yearicks for their many large and small acts of kindness during the span of this project. There are surely others whom we have inadvertently overlooked; with apologies, we thank them as well.

Finally, we note that this book would not have been possible without the artistic and graphic design talents of Dianne Mill and Susan Strohm of art270, Inc. The layout and design of the book is their creation. They have our great gratitude for the guidance they provided us and the patience with which they accepted our many modifications and changes.

An early copy of the alma mater of Beaver College. The same alma mater has been retained for Arcadia University. The phrase "Hail Arcadia" has been substituted for "Hail to Beaver". The words of the original were written in 1926 after the move to Jenkintown, Pa., by then College President, Lynn H. Harris. (Arcadia University Archives)

TABLE OF CONTENTS

Five of the gargoyles that decorate the facade of Grey Towers Castle. (Photos by David DeBalko, Huntingdon Valley, Pa.; Arcadia University Archives)

Preface —

Since the minutes of the meetings of the Board of Trustees, as herein recorded, give no account of the origin of the Institution, a brief sketch of its history from the time of the earliest steps for its foundation down to the period when "the minutes" commence, may not be uninteresting to him who may seek to know how, and by whom, its foundations were laid.

In the year 1853, Rev. Matthew Simpson D.D., Bishop of the M.E. Church, himself formerly an earnest labourer in the cause of education, suggested the idea of organizing a "High School for Young Ladies" in the town of Beaver, in conversation with Rev. Joshua Monroe. The project was at once received with favor, and, in view of the fact that there was then no school of this description within many miles of Beaver, and, in view of the many advantages which the location presented, its ease of access, its healthy atmosphere and beauty of scenery and the high moral and intellectual tone of its inhabitants, the more the idea was revolved the more feasible and attractive the project seemed. Resolved to put the matter to a practical test, Mr Monroe drew up a Subscription paper which, with a forethought which was afterwards found to avoid much difficulty and dispute, definitely located the "new school" in the Borough of Beaver"; and presented the paper to many citizens for their support. The plan met with much encouragement and many liberal subscriptions were obtained. Upon presenting the paper to Hon. D. Agnew, he suggested that a higher aim be taken and that instead of being merely a High School the new Institution should assume the character of a Female Seminary, with Chartered rights, upon a permanent basis and a large scale. In furtherance of this object Mr. Agnew subscribed $200 upon condition that $2500 be obtained. Many of the former subscribers now doubled their subscriptions and many new ones were obtained. A mass meeting was held, a Charter of Incorporation applied for, and a committee appointed to select a lot for the building. At a subsequent meeting of the subscribers a Board of Trustees was elected and the Rev J. K. Miller appointed to act as agent in procuring funds for the Seminary. By his exertions the fund was raised to $3500, and with this, the work of building was commenced, a Building Committee having been appointed by the Board of Trustees.

From this time forth, the following minutes afford the best history of the progress of the Institution, its difficulties and dangers and its final complete success. To those men who, in the Board of Trustees, have faithfully labored for its interests from its beginning until the present time, much honor is due. Long may the Institution stand as a monument to their liberality and that energy which no difficulties can daunt.

O. S. L.

The preface to the minutes of the Beaver Female Seminary's Board of Trustees, written in 1853. (Arcadia University Archives)

ix

FROM FEMALE SEMINARY TO COMPREHENSIVE UNIVERSITY[1]

PART I: THE SEMINARY AND EARLY COLLEGE 1853–1894

Ruth L. Higgins and Mary S. Sturgeon

The editors of *The Oxford English Dictionary* (1989) note, "In the earlier half of the 19th century, 'Seminary for Young Ladies' was very common as the designation of a private school for girls." *The Cyclopedia of Education: A Dictionary of Information* (1877) states that the term seminary was most often applied to secondary schools.

[1] This essay, and the two later essays by these authors, is excerpted from "Beaver College—the First Hundred Years" by Ruth L. Higgins, Dean of the College and Professor of History and Government, and Mary S. Sturgeon, Assistant Professor of English. The larger work was originally published in the *Journal of the Beaver College Alumnae Association*, Vol. XXX, No. 2, January 1954. The footnotes, explanatory notes, most of the illustrations, and captions have been added to this present version.

1872 view of Beaver College and Musical Institute. (Beaver Area Historical Museum)

THE SEMINARY AND
EARLY COLLEGE 1853–1894

Beaver College was founded as a Female Seminary in 1853. At the time there were few

seminaries or colleges open for young women. Numerous private academies for boys were

flourishing and colleges for young men had existed since 1636 when Harvard was founded . . . .

Women were not thought to have a capacity for intellectual pursuits equal to that of men; hence the education of girls was usually limited to reading, writing, a smattering of French, drawing, painting, music, and embroidery. Such subjects as Latin, Greek, and Mathematics were deemed beyond the mental grasp of young ladies. Three courageous women had served as pioneers in developing institutes with intellectual subjects for young women. Emma Willard had established a seminary at Troy, New York, in 1821; Mary Lyon in Mount Holyoke in 1836; and Catherine Beecher was responsible for a succession of female institutes at Hartford, Cincinnati, and Milwaukee, the last of which by 1851 had developed into the Milwaukee College. Colleges for women with standards comparable to those for men did not exist . . . .

The founders of Beaver Female Seminary, however, were men [2]. A former schoolman, the Reverend Matthew Simpson, Bishop of the Methodist Episcopal Church, in a conversation with the Reverend Joshua Monroe, proposed the idea of a "High School for Young Ladies" to be established in the Borough of Beaver. This quiet town

was chosen because of its accessibility in the beautiful Ohio valley, its healthful atmosphere, and "the high moral and intellectual tone of its inhabitants." Mr. Monroe drew up a subscription paper [a list of potential donors] and urged many citizens to give their support. When the Honorable Daniel Agnew (later president of the Board of Trustees and at one time Chief Justice of the State) was approached, he recommended that the new institution not be merely a high school but a seminary with chartered rights. Agnew himself subscribed $200 on the condition that $25,000 be obtained. Some of the first subscribers were inspired to double their subscriptions and many new ones were found. Application for a charter of incorporation for a "Seminary of Learning for the education of female youths in the Arts, Sciences and useful literature" was granted [by Beaver County on] December 28, 1853, and a board of trustees was elected. In a short time, $3,500 had been raised and a building projected, with the Reverend

[2] The charter members were: Reverend Joshua Munroe, Richard P. Roberts, Rev. J. Keiss Miller, Hiram Stowe, Benjamin Adams, William Henry, John Barcley, David Minus, J. J. Anderson, William Barnes, John Allison, Reverend William G. Taylor, William Anderson, John West, and L. Whitsell.

Bishop Matthew Simpson was one of the founders of the Beaver Female Seminary. He also was one of the founders of Pittsburgh Female College, another Methodist affiliated institution, with which Beaver College eventually merged. (Beaver Area Historical Museum)

The Honorable Daniel Agnew, influential in the formation of the Seminary, was one of its largest stockholders. An early member of the Board of Trustees of Beaver Female Seminary, he succeeded Joshua Monroe as Board President in 1865 and continued in that capacity until 1887. He was an active and ardent abolitionist and supporter of the Union cause: in 1863 he was elected to the Pennsylvania Supreme Court on the pro-Union Republican ticket, defeating his anti-Union Democratic opponent. He was elected Chief Justice in 1873, serving until his retirement in 1879 at age 70. (Beaver Area Historical Museum)

Beaver Female Seminary.

THIS Institution will open its first and summer term on the first Wednesday of May. Boarding Pupils will be accommodated in the Seminary building under the care of the Principal and Lady, at the rate of $50 per session, which secures to them

Board, Light and Lodging.

Pupils living contigious, and not desiring to enter as regular bonders, may dine in the Seminary at the rate of $1,25 per week.

The tuition fee will range, according to the studies pursued, from $6 to $12 per term of five months.

The services of Mrs. F. Wishart, well known as an efficient teacher, of long experience, have been secured.

The preparatory classes will, for the most part, be placed under the tuition of Miss A. M. Jones.

Mr. R. Leonhart, Professor of Music and Modern Languages, will take charge of the classes in Vocal and Instrumental Music.

The advanced classes will be placed under the instruction of the Principal. The domestic department will be under the superintendence of Mrs E. J. Baker.

With this board of Teachers, the Principal flatters himself that he will be able to meet the most sanguine expectations of the friends and patrons of the school.

All the ornamental branches will be taught in the Seminary, at usually low rates

Prof. Leonhart hopes to be able to give private instruction in music, languages and drawing to such as may not desire to enter the institution as regular pupils. For further instruction address the Principal.

April 30, 1856.   S. BAKER, Principal.

An advertisement that appeared in the April 30, 1856 *The Beaver Argus* soliciting students for the new Beaver Female Seminary. (Arcadia University Archives)

Beaver, Pennsylvania, 1859. Founded in 1802, Beaver is situated on a plateau on the north bank of the Ohio River about 26 miles northwest of Pittsburgh. As county seat, it has little industry and consists mainly of shops, offices, churches and homes. In the middle of the 19th century, when Beaver Female Seminary was founded, the population was slightly over 1,000 and the setting was largely pastoral. (Engraving by Emil Bott; Beaver Area Historical Museum)

3

Reverend Joshua Monroe was a founder of Beaver Female Seminary and first President of its Board of Trustees. He exerted considerable influence and leadership within the Pittsburgh Conference of the Episcopal Methodist Church. In 1854, when 65 years old, he retired to Beaver, Pennsylvania, where he became a justice of the peace and served for many years as the President of the Board of the new Seminary. (Beaver Area Historical Museum)

Colonel Richard P. Roberts was one of the founders of Beaver Female Seminary and served as Secretary of its first Board of Trustees. A lawyer, he was very active in civic affairs and was one of the leaders of the local abolitionists. In 1862 he helped organize and was appointed Colonel of the 140th Pennsylvania Volunteers. He was killed leading his regiment during the Battle of the Wheat Fields at Gettysburg on July 2, 1863. (Beaver Area Historical Museum)

STOCK FINANCED EDUCATIONAL CORPORATIONS

An early method of fundraising for educational institutions was to form a corporation and sell shares of stock in it. Interest often was paid on these shares. As in all publicly owned corporations, ownership of stock entitled the individual to attend an annual meeting of stockholders and to vote on changes in corporate policy and on the selection of trustees. Originally, the two major shareholders in the Beaver Female Seminary were Daniel Agnew and The Harmony Society (a utopian religious community). Individuals who bought shares amounting to more than $1,000 were made Life Trustees. Eventually, the Pittsburgh Conference of the Episcopal Methodist Church became a major shareholder and was guaranteed representation on the Board of Trustees.

The Corporation owned the grounds and buildings of the institution and, as was the case at Beaver, leased the building to the Principal or President of the Faculty. That individual collected all student fees and out of that income paid salaries to him- or herself and to the faculty members. All equipment, apparatus and supplies also were bought out of this income. The President assumed the business risk of the operation. After President Taylor's tenure, the President was paid a salary; the Board of Trustees set all salaries of faculty and staff and all payments of bills had to be approved by the Board which met monthly. As a result, the Board of Trustees now assumed the business risk. If a deficit was encountered, the Board had to either raise money or borrow money to cover the operating deficit. The system of stock-ownership was dissolved when Beaver College merged with The Beechwood School in 1925. *Samuel M. Cameron*

One of Joshua Monroe's Beaver Female Seminary stock certificates. (Beaver Area Historical Museum)

W. G. Taylor, Presbyterian minister and member of the board, as chief agent for the plans. This structure of brick, with flat roof and parapet walls, three stories high in addition to attic and stone basement above ground, containing kitchen, laundry, and dining room, was completed by the fall of 1855. The charter of 1853 and its amendment of 1855 provided for a corporation of stockholders with authority to choose the trustees and the principal. The latter was to be always a "regular member, in good standing, of the Methodist Episcopal Church." In 1854 the elected officers of the Board included the Reverend Joshua Monroe, president; Richard P. Roberts, secretary; and Benjamin Adams, treasurer [3].

Plans were made to open the seminary on May 7, 1856, but not until April 3 was the first principal elected, the Reverend Sheridan Baker, who came from the Brownsville School. His contract called for only three hundred dollars assistance from the trustees in furnishing the new building. On April 12, even before the opening, a windstorm tore off the cupola and portions of the tin roof and the chimneys, and eight hundred dollars had to be raised for repairs. Somehow these were completed for the opening on schedule.

At the first commencement, held in September, the usual closing time for female institutions in those days, the first two diplomas were awarded to the Misses Sylvania Jones and Juliet A. Poundstone, who with several other students had accompanied Principal Baker [from Brownsville] to the new seminary. The second class contained seven students. Perusal of one of the diplomas of September 1857 reveals the "masculine" quality of the curriculum even in this early time.

The second principal . . . was Professor Samuel Davenport, who assumed his duties upon the voluntary retirement of Sheridan Baker in 1858. Because of the indebtedness continuing to weigh heavily on the institution, the trustees decided to look about for someone who would take the lease for a [longer] term . . . .

Thus, in 1859, the Reverend Riley Treadway Taylor, the man whose influence and leadership were to give the seminary and later the college their distinctive quality, became principal. Dr. Taylor, holder of the A.B. and A.M. from Wesleyan University, and a member of Phi Beta Kappa, was a highly successful teacher of languages in the recently founded (1854) Pittsburgh Female College and formerly a secondary school administrator. He agreed to lease the Beaver Female Seminary for a term of ten years for $100 yearly; to pay the interest on a $1,000 loan negotiated by the trustees; to insure the building for at least $1,000; and to pay in furniture, equipment, or improvements on the buildings $5 per year for each boarding pupil exceeding twenty. Dr. Taylor requested the trustees to make application to court for

[3] The first Board of Trustees consisted of Joshua Monroe, President, Richard P. Roberts, Secretary, Benjamin Adams, Treasurer, Hiram Stowe, William G. Taylor, John Murray, Hugh Anderson, George W. Allison, and David Minus.

a charter change to admit boys. The final decree from this request (1860) provided that the name of the school be changed to "Beaver Seminary and Institute" and that from time to time, as seemed advisable, male pupils not exceeding fourteen years be admitted.

On November 2, 1859, the first term under Dr. Taylor's auspices opened with the entire Board present and the boarding department [i.e., resident students] greatly increased to 147 pupils. Music . . . , became the charge of one devoted to it and already a successful teacher, the charming and accomplished Amelia Spencer Taylor, wife of the principal.

By 1860 the enrollment of nearly 200 testified to the growing reputation of the institution. To be sure, many of these were local students in preparatory departments. For the next three years the building was filled to more than capacity. No rooms were available for servants, pianos had to be placed in students' rooms, and the principal's family of four had to live in one room. Fear of a loss of capacity enrollment under discomfort from the crowding of eighty-five people into the twenty-seven rooms above the basement grew and proved not groundless. As it was later remarked, "Lack of room cost Beaver ten years of its growth." But a lack of capital and industry in the borough of Beaver seemed an insurmountable obstacle to adequate support for the Seminary.

Dr. Taylor, after 1860 listed as president, on his own credit, however, began the erection of a president's house on the square opposite the original building. In 1865 the proprietor of the rival Main Street Female Seminary proposed to sell his building to Dr. Taylor for $10,500. The President accepted, mortgaging everything he had, and with better facilities (the original building having been planned without provision for recitation and practice rooms) and increasing confidence, Beaver Seminary and Institute grew rapidly. A Professor of Music was employed, and by 1865 the name of the institution was changed again, this time to Beaver Female Seminary and Musical Institute. For a year money was plentiful and pupils many, the total for 1865–1866 being 354. In 1866 the recently acquired building, situated at an inconvenient distance from the original one, was sold to a gentleman who opened a rival school. Further, public schools were being improved with the result that local patronage notably decreased. To compensate, males continued to be admitted to the Seminary as preparatory students.

The Catalogue of 1865–1866, one of the earliest available, claims for the Seminary that "In the extent of its English and Classical courses it invites comparison with any female school in the country, and in the thoroughness of its classes it challenges comparison with any school, male or female." Testimony of those who came under Dr. Taylor's instruction declared that his genuine scholarship and personal magnetism were most instrumental in making this statement no idle boast. The classics and English were the only emphases until 1860,

The diploma of Miss Lucy Letherman, class of 1857. Graduation was granted to young women who "had passed a creditable Examination in the following sciences . . . History, ancient and modern, Geography, ancient and modern, and Modern English Grammar, Arithmetic, Algebra, Geometry, including nine books of Legendre, Natural Philosophy, Chemistry, Physiology, Geology, Botany, Astronomy, Rhetoric, Logic, Intellectual Philosophy, Moral Science, Butler's Analogy and Natural Theology." Adrian Legendre was a 19th-century French mathematician whose work on algebra and geometry formed the basis of standard textbooks in those fields at that time. (Photo by Jerome Lukowicz, Philadelphia, Pa.; Arcadia University Archives)

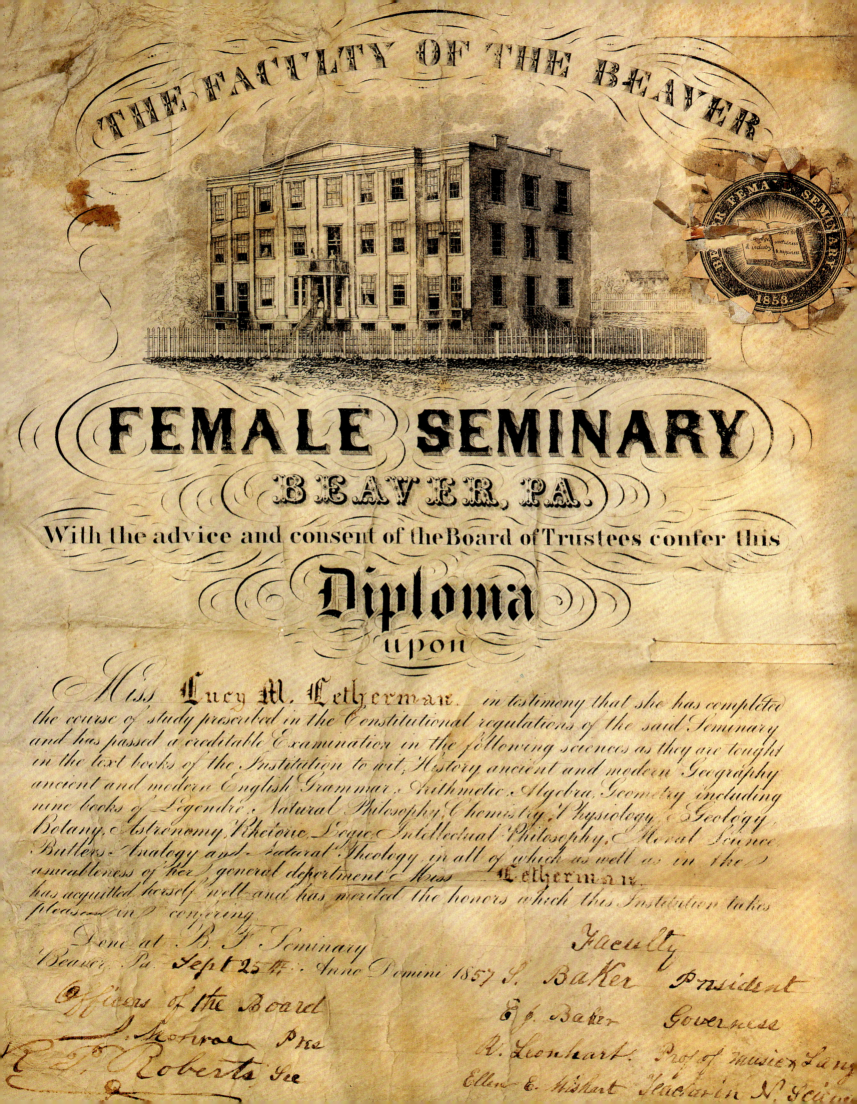

THE FACULTY OF THE BEAVER

FEMALE SEMINARY

BEAVER, PA.

With the advice and consent of the Board of Trustees confer this

Diploma

upon

Miss *Lucy M. Letherman* in testimony that she has completed the course of study prescribed in the Constitutional regulations of the said Seminary and has passed a creditable Examination in the following sciences as they are taught in the text books of the Institution to wit, History ancient and modern, Geography ancient and modern, English Grammar, Arithmetic, Algebra, Geometry including nine books of Legendre, Natural Philosophy, Chemistry, Physiology, Geology, Botany, Astronomy, Rhetoric, Logic, Intellectual Philosophy, Moral Science, Butlers Analogy and Natural Theology in all of which as well as in the amiableness of her general deportment Miss *Letherman* has acquitted herself well and has merited the honors which this Institution takes pleasure in conferring.

Done at B. F. Seminary
Beaver, Pa. Sept 25th Anno Domini 1857

Officers of the Board

J. Monroe Pres

R. P. Roberts Sec

Faculty

S. Baker President

E. J. Baker Governess

R. Leonhart Prof of music & Lang

Ellen E. Wishart Teacher in N. Sci

President Taylor's private residence, Sunnydale, with Mrs. Taylor cutting flowers in the foreground. The women standing by the building are probably daughters Carolyn and Julie. (Arcadia University Archives)

Examination of Beaver College,

TUESDAY MORNING, JUNE 25, '72

9:00.—Arithmetic D. ....Miss Woodroffe.

Inst. Duett—Warblings at Eve. (*Richards*) Misses URLING and HOLMES.

9:45.—General History...Miss Magee.

BALLAD.." 'Twas but a dream." (*Lyons*.)...........................Class No. 3.

Misses Smith, Horton, Raiff, Stiles, Jennings & McFarland.

10:20.— Higher Arithmetic, ...Prof. Townsend.

PIANO SOLO—Polonaise Brilliante. (*Oesten*.)..... ....Miss Augustine.

11.15.—Telemachus................................. .. ..Miss Burnett.

BALLAD—"I cannot sing that song to-night." (*Demings*) Miss Clarke.

SONG—"Home Again." (*Ordway*.)..........................Private Class No. 3.

Misses Grist, McFarland, Barr, Shugert, Beacom, Taylor, Richardson and Goff.

Tuesday Afternoon.

1.15.—GRAMMAR—B........ ....Prof. Dunlap.

PIANO SOLO—Polka di Bravvre. (*Kunn*.)......................Miss Morton.

ESSAY...................................Miss Ida Harden, *Wheeling, West Va.*

2:10—PHYSIOLOGY..Miss Burnett.

DECLAMATION—(William Tell)........... ....GEORGE WALTERS

ESSAY—Miss RAY C. GIST................................ *Williamsburg, West Va.*

VOC. SOLO & DUETT—"Under the snow.'' (*Sherratt*)—
Misses RAIFF and SMITH.

3;10.—BOTANY..... ....Prof. TOWNSEND.

RECITATION—Miss ANNIE BEACOM.

SONG—"La Notta e Bella." (*Guglielmo*.)........................Private Class No. 1

Misses Gist, Urling, Miller, McCormick, Morton and Patterson.

PAPER —................................. ...CHARLES WHISLER, *Bolesville, Pa.*

PIANO DUETT—Grande Valse. *Schulhoff*.) Misses FOSTER & MORTON.

COMMENCEMENT CONCERT......Evening; at the M. E. Church......at 8 o'clock.

Receipt to Mr. S. H. Darragh for his daughter's tuition for the 1883 winter session. (Arcadia University Archives)

but by 1865 the Institute for instruction in music was established, where those desiring to could devote themselves exclusively to its study "without being compelled to journey East" . . . . "Much more than the usual attention" was given to painting and drawing, "those beautiful and refining branches of ornamental study," and "healthful and delightful calisthenic exercises [were] taught to all pupils without extra charge." Normal courses for teachers were conducted in academic subjects as well as in music.

BEAVER COLLEGE AND MUSICAL INSTITUTE

The year 1872 was a momentous one in the history of Beaver, the new charter of that year authorizing the change from a Seminary to a "College for the education of both sexes, in all the branches of learning usually taught in the Colleges and Seminaries of the United States, and also in such fine arts as may be authorized by the board of trustees" and empowering it to confer the appropriate degrees. The inclusion of "Musical" in the new name, Beaver College and Musical Institute, indicated the purpose and charter authority to cultivate music as an art and science.

By 1875 three courses of study were established: the Classical leading to the degree of Mistress of Liberal Arts[4] (M.L.A.); the English course leading to the degree of Mistress of English Literature (M.L.L.); and a Boys' Preparatory course. Diplomas were awarded to those completing the courses in music and painting, and plans

were also proposed for a teacher training class under the instruction of Dr. Taylor. In 1875 the first recorded honorary degree was awarded, a Mistress of Liberal Arts. Of the seven degrees awarded in 1884 by a faculty of eleven, four were Masters of Art.

A list of subjects taught in the early college indicates that few if any concessions were made to the then popular fallacy that women were intellectually not capable of following a curriculum such as prevailed in colleges for men. In addition to Latin and Greek, together with music the most stressed studies in the college, the courses included Algebra, French, German, Rhetoric, English Literature, Elocution, History of Rome, Higher Arithmetic, Natural Philosophy (Physics), Uranography [i.e., charting of heavenly bodies], United States Constitution, Physical Geography, Geometry, Mental Philosophy (Psychology), Book-Keeping, Zoology, Trigonometry, Chemistry, Astronomy, and Geology.

By 1893, "determined to be abreast of the times" the College was furnished with "philosophical and chemical" apparatus to which additions were made from time to time . . . . In its observatory a telescope provided "sufficient power to reveal all the more common, and to the general student, more interesting phenomena of the heavens" . . . .

---

[4] Mistress degrees were equivalent to bachelors degrees, but awarded to women. The masters degree, by contrast, was a genuine postgraduate degree in the modern sense.

Development of the Campus

By the late sixties the need for better teaching facilities again was pressing in spite of the erection of a frame building for boys near the principal's residence. At the Commencement of 1871 John F. Dravo, long the friend and financial "Ajax Major" [i.e., hero] at Beaver, who had been attracted to the town by the institution and had already expressed his generosity to it, gave life to the project of a new building with a gift of $10,000. During the year 1871–1872 subscriptions were sought for a school building to cost $27,000 with the exception of furnaces, and by the fall of 1872 a building nearly twice as large as the first one was enclosed.

The original building had already been improved in style when a new roof to replace the tin one had become a necessity. Now, to this structure by simple alteration in one end was attached another, including spacious recitation and practice rooms and a College Hall seating four hundred. From this time to the fire in 1896, this hall served the town as well as the College as a place of assembly. No longer were the college members obliged to go to the church for public exercises, transporting even the piano.

One of the subscribers was unable to meet his subscription of $10,000 because of business reverses, but the Trustees determined to carry on and College Hall was dedicated at the commencement of 1873. With the panic of 1873 plainly at hand, it was left to Dr. Taylor personally to put in the furnace for heating and furniture for the school rooms and the additional boarders' rooms. Nearly twenty years passed before the debt was entirely removed and not until the president had paid out of the institution $10,000 in interest—all of which should have gone, lamented Dr. Taylor, into the improvement and elevation of the college. As late as 1885, in spite of pleas and plans and even jug-filling by loyal alumnae, the college debt was still $5,500 . . . .

[College Hall] stood in a two-acre plot enclosed by a high board fence except for a space immediately in front where gratings [i.e., a picket fence] allowed students to be abroad unchaperoned . . . . Rooms were inspected regularly. Lights were officially off at 10 p.m., but even then the students found ways to study after hours.

Student Life in the Taylor Era

In the dining room each student was required to furnish her own silver and napkins. After each meal she washed her silver, wrapped it in a napkin, and placed it in her own room (later on a shelf) where she picked it up on her way to the next meal. After dinner Dr. Taylor gave advice on the general rules of life, commented on current events, and called upon Divine guidance.

At the Methodist Church all students sat together in the "Amen corner" under the unobstructed eye of the President and his family in their pew at the center of the church. Sunday afternoon from two to three o'clock was "Meditation Hour" when the students remained in their

John F. Dravo, President of the Board of Trustees (1887–1905) and major benefactor. (Beaver Area Historical Museum)

continued on page 17

The Senior Class of
Beaver College and Musical Institute
requests your presence at the
Commencement Exercises,
Thursday evening, June seventh 1888,
at eight o'clock.
Beaver, Pa.

"Multa ferunt anni venientes, commoda secum."

Iney I. Armstrong,	Laura Hice,
Minnie K. Allemong,	May Kells
Lenora I. Berry,	Phoebe F. Kennedy,
Harriet D. Calhoon,	Anna L. Latshaw,
Mary S. Endsley,	Ada Lee Mapel,
Mary W. Gardner	Eliza F. Patterson,
	Evalyn L. Patterson,

No flowers.

E.A.WRIGHT, PHILA.

Invitation of the Class of
1888 to its Commencement
exercises on June 7, 1888.
(Arcadia University Archives)

The Class of 1888.
(Arcadia University Archives)

Senator Matthew S. Quay.
(Beaver Area
Historical Museum)

Congressional Medal of Honor.
(From the collections of the
Spruance Library of the Bucks
County Historical Society)

MATTHEW S. QUAY, THE "KING MAKER"

The Honorable Matthew S. Quay, United States Senator, was a member of the Beaver College Board of Trustees from 1873 through 1884 and a Life Trustee from 1885 until his death on May 28, 1904.

Quay's father was a prominent Presbyterian minister who was the pastor at the Beaver Presbyterian Church. Matthew married Agnes Barclay, daughter of the Honorable John Barclay, one of the original incorporators of Beaver Female Seminary and a Board member from 1855 to 1867.

After studying law with Colonel Richard Roberts (a founder and Secretary of the Board of Trustees of Beaver Female Seminary) and being admitted to the Beaver County Bar, Quay was appointed Prothonotary of the County. In 1861, when the Civil War began, he resigned his office and enlisted in the Tenth Pennsylvania Reserves as a lieutenant and eventually was promoted to Colonel of the 134th Regiment of the Pennsylvania Volunteers. He was mustered out of the army because of ill health, but learning that his regiment was about to enter battle within a few days, stayed and, as a volunteer, led the charge on Marye's Heights in the battle of Fredericksburg on December 13, 1862. He was awarded the Congressional Medal of Honor for his participation in this battle. The citation states, "Although out of service, he voluntarily resumed duty on the eve of battle and took a conspicuous part in the charge on the heights." The medal was not awarded until July 9, 1888, twenty-three years after the end of the war. Many Congressional Medals of Honor were awarded after the Civil War for political purposes and Quay's medal may have been won more for his political than for his military successes.

Quay continued to serve as Pennsylvania State Military Secretary, a civilian position, until the end of the war when he entered politics. He was first elected to the State Legislature and became Chairman of the Republican State Committee and a member of the Republican National Committee. He eventually ran for and was elected to the United States Senate in 1887. As head of the Pennsylvania delegation at the Republican National Convention in 1888, he played a pivotal role in the nomination of and, later, the election of Benjamin Harrison as President of the United States. His role in this triumph earned him the nickname, "The King Maker." *Samuel M. Cameron*

Sources
History of Beaver County, Pennsylvania. (1888). Philadelphia and Chicago: A. Warner & Co.
Matthew Stanley Quay. (1970). Beaver, Pa.: Beaver County Tourist Promotion Agency.

The original building with
its new roof added in 1868.
(Beaver Area Historical Museum)

Residence hall room
around 1890.
(Arcadia University Archives)

Dr. Taylor with female students
in Sunday attire. (Beaver Area
Historical Museum)

The College library during Taylor era. (Beaver Area Historical Museum)

rooms with no visitors. Not until after the departure of the Taylors was there such a thing as a dance at Beaver, although on Friday nights, after the Literary Society meetings, the girls might dance together. At least one teacher objected to even this, claiming it would tempt the girls sometimes to dance with men.

Daily walks with a chaperone were a diversion. The most significant activity in the life of the College, however, and of great attraction to the town, was the Literary Societies, for most of the time the Parthenon and the Owlets, meeting alternately on Friday nights. Every student belonged to one of these societies, whose programs consisted of music, readings, current news, and debates. Always a critic was appointed and club rivalry gave zest to the occasions.

Students of the earliest Beaver, like students of the present, also had their "things required and things prohibited."

In 1877 school dress was advised if not prescribed to be no longer than the "modern walking skirt, loose and suspended from the shoulders, as all cloths should be, thus securing opportunity for the development of the chest and for full respirations without which the vigor of health cannot long be maintained." According to the Catalogue of 1882–1883, school authorities recommended that pupils wear a dress with a loose plaited waist, navy blue color preferred, "inexpensive, and the only dress needed except one for church." By this means it was

thought "to prevent display and diversion of the mind from the great object of school life." Parents were earnestly requested not to permit their children to have more than the bare minimum of spending money, or to bring jewelry, which was not allowed to be worn for display.

Enthusiasm for music overflowed the lesson and practice rooms into various music organizations such as The St. Cecelia Society and Chorus. Programs were popular with townspeople as well as the college family although the composers represented were chiefly the classical ones. A college orchestra, described in a tribute in verse as "glorious and fine," flourished at least in the 1880s.

In 1878 appeared the first issue of *The College Messenger*, a bi-monthly news-magazine named for the popular "College Messenger" formerly prepared for the Friday evening exercises of the literary societies. The back page of each issue carried an advertisement of the college, and within appeared not only accounts of "doings" and events of especial interest to the college and its immediate friends but also surprisingly mature and sober articles on various topics of "an educational character."

In the pages of *The College Messenger* of June 1884, we find the first record of a May Day celebration. The entertainment, described as "one of the most charming ever given by the institution," was attended by a "richly dressed, quite select audience." The hall was beautifully decorated with myrtle and evergreens and a multi-colored maypole, the attraction of the evening as it was twined

RULES AND REGULATIONS.

THINGS REQUIRED.

1. A diligent employment of time.
2. Prompt and punctual performance of duty.
3. Strict observance of school and study hours.
4. Order and neatness of rooms.
5. Cleanliness of person and neatness of apparel.
6. Propriety and decorum at table.
7. Careful management of lights and fuel.
8. A strict observance of the Sabbath.
9. Attendance at Church twice, and Bible Class or Sunday School, each Sabbath.
10. Promptness in rising and retiring when the signal is given.
11. Reporting and settling for any article of furniture damaged or destroyed.
12. Obedience and due respect to teachers.

THINGS PROHIBITED.

1. Visiting in school or study hours.
2. Unnecessary noise in rooms or halls.
3. Entering each other's rooms without permission of occupants.
4. Lounging on the beds during the day.
5. Calling or conversing from the windows.
6. Throwing anything from windows or porches.
7. Sending notes, letters or parcels by day pupils or other persons, without permission.
8. Reading, writing, or labor not connected with the school duties in school or study hours.
9. Borrowing or lending articles of clothing or money.
10. Leaving the Seminary grounds without permission.
11. Writing more than one letter each week without permission.
12. Being absent from school or recitation.
13. Washing or ironing in boarders' rooms.

Rules and regulations as stated in the 1865–1866 catalog. (Arcadia University Archives)

by eight "queens" who in beautiful attire "performed their revolutions in an exceedingly graceful manner." Music, instrumental and vocal, completed the "delightful social time enjoyed by all."

The End of the Taylor Era

The beneficent reign of Dr. Taylor came to an end in 1894. Preparation for this change was begun with the election in July of 1893 of the Reverend Appleton Bash of the Pittsburgh Conference as associate president of the college. In December the trustees voted to assume greater control, to purchase the school equipment then owned by Dr. Taylor, to elect the president and faculty, to determine the course of study, and to establish by-laws and regulations. The tenor of the minutes reflects a disappointment of the trustees in the unprosperous condition of the college, both academically and otherwise, and a willingness to accept much of the blame for their carelessness in leaving almost everything to the president.

At a meeting in February of 1894, Dr. Taylor offered to terminate the disagreement between an appointed committee and himself over a price for the furniture and equipment belonging to him by permitting the trustees themselves to fix the price. He then tendered his resignation, to take effect at commencement in June. The resignation accepted, Professor W. J. Alexander was nominated for President for three years at an annual salary of $2,000.

THIRTY=NINTH

COMMENCEMENT

BEAVER COLLEGE
AND MUSICAL INSTITUTE

Wednesday, Eve., June 20, 1894.

PROGRAMME.

Piano Solo—Sarabande.........................WILM
Miss Mary Kidney, Allegheny.

Essay—Salutatory—"Pandora's Box,"..................
Miss Grace G. Holmes, Columbus, Ohio.

Vocal Solo—The End of the Story...........WEATHERBY
Miss Blanche Bray, Industry, Pa.

Essay—Signs of the Times....................... .....
Miss Lyda A. Bonner, Stoneboro.

Vocal Solo—Beautie's Eyes....................FERBER
Miss Jessie Galey, Beaver, Pa.

Oration—Books................................
Miss Mary L. Foley, Allegheny.

Piano Solo— { a. Arabeske..........MEYER HELMUND
{ b. Faschingsschwank.........SCHUMANN
Miss Julia Berry Taylor, College.

Essay—Architecture............................
D. Josephine Davis, McKeesport.

Vocal Solo—Wilt Thou Sorrow,..........DER FREISCHUTZ
Miss Cora F. Strickler, Wilkinsburg.

Essay—Yesterday, To-day and To-morrow.............
Miss Lina T. Armentrout, Mt. Vernon, O.

Harp—The Last Rose of Summer................BACHSE
Mrs. Gilbert, College.

Essay and Valedictory—La Belle Rivere................
Miss Mary Elise Calhoon, Georgetown.

Address to the Graduates by the President.

Conferring Degrees.

Vocal Solo— { a. My Little Love...............HAWLEY
{ b. At Parting...................ROGERS
Mrs. Henry C. Fry, Rochester.

The program for the 39th Annual Commencement of Beaver College and Musical Institute, President Taylor's last. (Arcadia University Archives)

RUDYARD KIPLING VISITS MUSQUASH ON THE MONONGAHELA

AN ESSAY

Samuel M. Cameron

Rudyard Kipling. (Beaver Area Historical Museum)

Edmonia Taylor Hill. (Beaver Area Historical Museum)

In the summer of 1889, Rudyard Kipling was a guest of President Taylor and his family at Beaver College. Kipling visited Beaver during his trip around the world, which he described in *From Sea to Sea: Letters of Travel*. Of all the places he visited in the United States, he seemed to enjoy "the infinite peace of the tiny township" of Beaver, Pennsylvania, the best. "Imagine a rolling, wooded, English landscape, under the softest of blue skies, dotted at three-mile intervals with fat little, quiet little villages, or aggressive little manufacturing towns that the trees and the folds of the hills mercifully prevented from betraying their presence . . . . It was good to lie in a hammock with half-shut eyes, and, in the utter stillness, to hear the apples dropping from the trees, and the tinkle of the cowbells as the cows walked stately down the main road of the village." Despite his appreciation of the town relative to the rest of the United States, Kipling could not totally control his cynical acerbic tongue and, in order to protect the feelings of his hosts, disguised the identity of the town by calling it "Musquash," an American Indian name for a beaver, and moved the town up the Ohio River to the Monongahela. How did Kipling come to visit the Taylors and this idyllic, but tiny, town and obscure college?

The story begins when Kipling graduated from the United Services College in Westward Ho, England, at the age of 16, and instead of going on to university, decided to rejoin his family in India and start a career as a journalist. His father was Principal of the Mayo School of Art and Curator of the Lahore Museum in Lahore, India. Through family contacts, Kipling landed a job as a reporter for the *Civil and Military Gazette*. In 1887, at age 22, he joined the *Gazette's* parent newspaper, the prestigious *Pioneer*, published in Allahabad.

In August 1884, after receiving her A.M. from Beaver College, Edmonia K. Taylor, the daughter of President Taylor, married Samuel Alec Hill, an English meteorologist who had recently been appointed Professor of Science at Muir University in Allahabad. The newly wed couple immediately traveled to India so that Professor Hill could assume his teaching responsibilities. They arrived on the 14th of October 1884, several years before Kipling transferred from Lahore to Allahabad. In the small English community living in Allahabad, it was inevitable that the Hills and Kipling would meet. Edmonia Hill was to become a close friend and confidant of young Kipling.

The two met at a dinner party at the house of George Allen, a publisher of the *Pioneer*. Edmonia described the meeting in a letter to her younger sister, Carolyn. "When we were seated at table and conversation was in full swing, my partner called my attention to a short dark-haired man of uncertain age, with a heavy moustache and wearing very thick glasses, who sat opposite, saying: 'That is Rudyard Kipling, who has just come from Lahore to be on the staff of the *Pi*. He is writing those charming sketches of the native states, *Letters of Marque*, which the *Pi* is publishing . . . .' After dinner, when the men joined the ladies in the drawing room, evidently the retiring young author had marked me for an American, and, seeking copy perhaps, he came to the fireplace where I was standing and began questioning me about my homeland . . . . He is certainly worth knowing, and we shall ask him to dinner soon."

A few weeks after their first meeting, Rudyard sent Edmonia a copy of his newly published *Plain Tales from the Hills* with a dedicatory verse: "Would they were worthier. That's too late—Framed pictures stand no further stippling. Forgive the faults. To Mrs. Hill, March '88. From Rudyard Kipling." Future writings during these India years, however, were sent to Edmonia before framing, for her opinion and comments.

Kipling biographers have speculated on the close relationship of these two people. There is no doubt that Kipling had a crush on Edmonia, and that part of his motivation for seeking her opinion of his writings was to get her attention and esteem. Kipling, up to his marriage, displayed considerable ambivalence about serious relationships with women other than his close relatives. His true affections were reserved for young women who were unattainable. His first engagement, to Florence (Flo) Garrad (he was 16, she 17 or 18), occurred as he was about to sail from England to India. Mrs. Hill, safely married, while not as distant as Flo, was equally unattainable. During her student years at Beaver College, Edmonia was a talented prize-winning artist and scholar. After graduation, she became a faculty member, teaching writing and supervising the student newspaper, *The Beaver*. She was naturally flattered by the value Kipling placed on her literary opinion. She found the witty, creative Kipling a source of intellectual stimulation in the tepid cultural environment of Allahabad. In a letter to her youngest sister, Julia, she writes, "We have become quite well acquainted and we both enjoy his cleverness . . . . " In addition she notes that both of his parents were prominent people in India and that his mother (like Edmonia) was the oldest daughter of a Methodist minister. That there might have been a little romantic interest is betrayed by her amusement and intrigue in his dalliances with other young women of whom he kept her posted. In a letter to Carolyn she observes, "Young Kipling is certainly all things to all people . . . . I hear he can make first-class love to the latest belle in Simla."

The friendship grew until eventually Kipling moved in with the Hills at their home "Belvedere." In a letter to the family Edmonia states, "We are discussing whether we should generously offer to take him in to our house for a little while rather than to let him go to the Club in this desolate season . . . . He would not be much trouble and might prove a pleasant companion." After explaining that because of landscaping improvements it would be impossible for him to stay in the separate bungalow, she proposed that he should stay in the main house. "R. can have the dressing room, bath, and east verandah, so he can be very comfortable . . . . The Blue Room has every convenience and is quite private, with its own verandah and entrance from the hall." Both the Hills and Kipling were away from Belvedere during the hot summer months, so in fact spent only brief periods of time together in the house.

Kipling wrote long gossipy letters to Edmonia. One recurrent topic was a supposed love affair he was having with "My Lady" for whom he declared an undying, but unrequited affection. In letter after letter he told Edmonia who "My Lady" was not, but never identified who she was. C.E. Carrington, one of Kipling's biographers, speculates, "The reader begins to suppose her a figment of the young writer's fancy, a projection, perhaps, of Mrs. Hill herself, to whom he must not declare his devotion."

Kipling wrote "The Man Who Would Be King" while living with the Hills. Edmonia tells the following story in a letter to Julia. "When 'The Man Who Would Be King' was germinating in R. K.'s mind he was lunching with us. Suddenly he demanded names for his characters. A. promptly said, 'Well, the queerest name I ever heard was that of a missionary I met in the Himalayas when we were both tramping—Peachy Taliaferro Wilson.' Of course Rudyard seized that at once. I could think of no name to give, so R. said, 'Well, who was the most prominent man in your home town?' Of course you know that I replied Mr. Dravo, and sure enough he used these very names, adding a *t* to Dravo." Mr. John Dravo was a prominent resident of the town of Beaver, a major benefactor of Beaver College and President of its Board of Trustees. Thus, the two adventurers in the tale were named Peachy Carnehan and Daniel Dravot.

In the fall of 1888, Edmonia became seriously ill with meningitis and, when she recovered, decided to recuperate at home in Beaver, Pennsylvania. Kipling also had been advised by his doctor to not spend another hot summer in India. He decided that he would return to England, but travel east, see the Orient, America, and visit with the Hills in Beaver. He talked his publisher into financing a series of travel articles for the *Pioneer*. He and the Hills booked passage on the same ship, the S.S. Madura of the British India line, and set sail from Calcutta to Rangoon on March 9, 1889. Kipling filed articles from Rangoon, Singapore, Hong Kong, Canton, and Japan. Along the way, Alec Hill took photographs and the three friends planned an illustrated travel book that never materialized. Instead, the series of newspaper reports were eventually published in Kipling's travelogue, *From Sea to Sea*. While Edmonia is not mentioned in these reports, Alec is; he is referred to as "The Professor." The photographs are now in an album in the Rare Book Collection of the Library of Congress. On May 11 the travelers sailed from Yokohama for San Francisco. Once they arrived in San Francisco, the Hills immediately headed by train for Beaver, while Kipling set out to see the United States. The reports he filed on the United States were highly critical in word and tone, inflaming the American press and public.

Young women playing
badminton at the College.
Kipling is reputed to have
introduced the sport to
the college community.
(Arcadia University Archives)

The only place in the United States about which Kipling had something good to say was Beaver, Pennsylvania, where Kipling rejoined his friends the Hills later in the summer. He was a guest of the Taylor family and was given rooms in the College dormitory. In a critical voice, Edmonia said, "He is settled in the rooms of the College, where he has a living room with open fireplace, a spacious bedroom and bath. There is a couch, where I think he spends most of his time, smoking, reading, and meditating, but not doing much writing." Kipling also had time for the young ladies of the town and is reputed to have introduced badminton to the College. The residents of the town still reminisce about his visit. Sixty-two years later, the *Beaver Falls News Tribune* of February 11, 1951, described the dinner party the Taylors gave to welcome Kipling, and their daughter and son-in-law. "An exciting garden party was held on the grounds of the house which was occupied by Edmonia's father. Japanese lanterns were strung from the home all the way to Third Street. Everyone was invited to attend and the guests were attired in dress suits and evening gowns. Caterers came from Pittsburgh and the waiters walked up from the station in their black suits. This caused quite a sensation in the town. Conversation, music, and excellent food added to the enjoyment." Edmonia wore an elaborate kimono of a dark fabric with embroidery in which were sewn the iridescent wings of beetles.

However, in the strict Methodist environment of the town, the party had no dancing or drinking. Beaver then, as now, was a "dry" town. A favorite tale is how Kipling still was able to obtain his daily glass of spirits. He obtained a prescription from a physician, and the College's janitor drove him each day in the Taylors' phaeton to the local druggist where Rudyard sipped his ration while relaxing in the carriage.

China decorating was very fashionable at the time and the College offered lessons in this art medium. Kipling developed the idea of writing some verses on dessert plates as a "thank you" gift to his hosts. Edmonia wrote in her diary for August 1889, "I've been painting a set of dessert plates with a design of our wild flowers to take back to India. One day Mr. Kipling, who has seemed unusually preoccupied, demanded china and paint. We wondered what project was being evolved in that fertile brain and now we know, for he has put upon six fruit plates some clever verses, about ten lines each, which he painted directly on the china without any notes . . . . They are rather badly painted in dark blue, as he was not accustomed to china paints and did not know how to use the turpentine. We tried to help, but he was too speedy for us." The Taylors used the plates as everyday dining ware. They are now housed in the Rare Book Room of the Library of Congress.

There was also a summer romance. Rudyard, apparently with the matchmaking instigation of Edmonia, carried on a flirtation with Carolyn Taylor. Edmonia was, perhaps, eager to divert some of Rudyard's attentions from herself to her younger sister. He wrote a short poem about Carolyn. Each of the fruit plates he created, on the reverse side, had some reference to her. On one are her initials, CAT; on another, a drawing of a cat; on still another, a drawing of the plant, cattails. The references to her on the plates have led some

Three of the six fruit plates on
which Kipling painted original
verses as a "thank you" gift
to his hosts. (Library of
Congress Rare Book Collection)

PLUMS

Children of ye Garden We
Simple and of low Degree.
Such as chuse Us ere our Time
Suffer Paines unmeet for Rhyme
Such as eat us overmuch
Suffer like ye other Such.
Purblind Race of toiling men
Lap Us round with Pye-Crust – then
Served with Sugar and with Cream
Ye shall find Us what we Seem.

THE PEACH

Ye Garden's royal Pride am I.
A Queen of Beauty manifold,
Y-clad in Crimson dasht with Golde
And crowned by every Summer Skie.
Take ye my Largesse Merrilie
Nor dread this Giving shall grow small.
Ye Trellis on ye Sun-warmed Wall
Hath hundreds not less Faire than I.

BERRIES

We be gamins of the Wood
Who claime the Bramble's brotherhood,
A feeble folk in russet dressed
Of all Earth's children littlest
The brown Bear knows us where we hide
By river-bank or mountain-side –
The settler's baby, brown as he,
Espies where our battalions be
And shameless peddles at the mart
Red jewels warm from Nature's heart

25

Edmonia in her kimono
with her sister Carolyn
in academic robes.
(Arcadia University Archives)

historians to suppose that Kipling created the plates for her. As the summer drew to an end, Professor Hill had to return to his teaching post in Allahabad. He left for India before his wife and Carolyn accompanied her sister on her journey back to India. Kipling met Edmonia and Carolyn in New York and sailed with them for London on September 25, 1889, on the ship *City of Berlin*. Kipling's romance with Carolyn continued and somewhere between New York and London the two became engaged. On October 9, Edmonia recorded in her diary, "Carrie engaged to R. K."

The engagement was to be short lived. Carolyn sailed with her sister for India on October 25, 1889. She, like Flo, became unattainable by distance. While he had been able to write long letters daily to Edmonia, he struggled to write to Carolyn. In one letter to Carolyn he says, "There lie in my waste paper basket the torn fragments of three long letters to you. Excellent letters they were but I destroyed 'em because I was afraid of the coldly critical eye that would read 'em. Heart o' mine you, as well as I, must have discovered by this time that the writing of love letters is no easy thing."

Carolyn Taylor. (Beaver Area Historical Museum)

Carolyn became uneasy about rumors of Kipling's lack of religious convictions and wrote asking him about them. He wrote a letter to reassure her of his belief in God; instead, the letter had the opposite effect on the devout Methodist. "Chiefly I believe in the existence of a personal God . . . . I disbelieve directly in eternal punishment for reasons that would take too long to put down on paper. On the same grounds I disbelieve in an eternal reward. As regards the mystery of the Trinity and the Doctrine of Redemption I regard them most reverently but cannot give them implicit belief, accepting them rather as dogmas of the Church than as matters that rush to the heart." One can imagine Carolyn, the daughter of a Methodist minister, being appalled and dismayed by this strange version of the Apostles' Creed. It is not clear who broke off the engagement, Carolyn or Rudyard, but their relationship ended shortly after this exchange of letters. Deepening the mystery is that sometime during this period he again met Flo Garrard, his first love. Did he deliberately create an estrangement with Carolyn in order to be free to once more pursue Flo?

Edmonia and Kipling did not correspond again for over ten years. During that time Kipling married Carolyn Balestier, the sister of his American friend, Wolcott. In the winter of 1899, both Kipling and his daughter, Josephine, became seriously ill with pneumonia. Kipling recovered, but his six-year-old daughter died. Following this loss, Edmonia wrote to him and they resumed their correspondence, though not with the same frequency and intensity of the years in India. Kipling died of a perforated ulcer on January 12, 1936. It was not till after his death that Edmonia published the above quoted letters and extracts from her diary about Kipling in the April 1936 issue of the *Atlantic Monthly*.

Sources
Carrington, C. E. (1955). *The life of Rudyard Kipling*. Garden City, NY: Doubleday & Company.
Hill, E. (1936, April). The young Kipling. *Atlantic Monthly*, *157*, 406–415.
Kenah, S. (1951, February). Come with me to Musquash. *News Tribune*. Beaver, Pa.
Kipling, R. (1899). *From sea to sea; Letters of travel*. New York: Doubleday & McClure Company.
Ricketts, H. (1999). *Rudyard Kipling: A life*. New York: Carroll & Graf Publishers.

FROM FEMALE SEMINARY TO COMPREHENSIVE UNIVERSITY

PART II: THE MATURING COLLEGE 1895–1924

Ruth L. Higgins and Mary S. Sturgeon

ALMA MATER
Down where flows the broad Ohio
Hills on every hand
Stands our college Alma Mater
Fairest in the land.

May her sons and daughters ever
Loyal be and true,
Firmly stand for God and country
All life's journey through.

Refrain:
Hail to Beaver! Hail to Beaver!
With glad hearts we say,
Hail to Beaver and her colors
Scarlet and the gray.

Beaver students on an outing at Beaver's Riverside Park on the bank of the Ohio River. (Arcadia University Archives)

THE MATURING COLLEGE
1895–1924

Immediately upon Dr. Taylor's retirement the College was reorganized, made truly

co-educational, and brought "fully abreast of modern preparatory Education." All records

suggest that for several years after the reorganization there was a slump in the level

of instruction and a shifting emphasis in kind.

The aim of the reorganized institution was stated as two-fold: "To prepare young men and women for our best Universities and Technical Schools, and for Professional and Business Life" . . . . The Board voted to institute an advanced academic course of study for four years and a preparatory course limited to two years. Physics and chemistry were also offered. A physics professor was elected at a salary of $550 and board and room, a professor of English and History at $500, a professor of art at $400 plus up to $100 of any excess from her classes, and a principal of the commercial department at $100 a month.

For the first time tuition was fixed by the Board: for those in the "solid branches" of the literary course, at $60 per year of three terms; tuition, board, room, and some laundry for boarding pupils at $250 for the year; tuition in German and French at $15 each term. In the preparatory department tuition was $10 per term with an extra charge for pupils in physics of $1.50 per year and for those in chemistry of $5 per year.

Then just as the college was entering upon its third term of the year, in February of 1895, the main building was completely destroyed by fire.[5] However, the "Circular" for 1895–1896 declares that not a single recitation or college exercise was lost or abridged in consequence of the fire, thanks to the generous assistance of the churches and schools of the town. Before the ashes were cold a new building was planned containing a hall, gymnasium, library, laboratories, and necessary classrooms for the successful handling of three hundred students, to be ready for occupancy September 16.

President Alexander was asked to resign in 1896,[6] to be succeeded by Professor N. H. Holmes of the Pittsburgh Female College. This year marked the consolidation of Beaver College with this sister college,

[5] See the essay, "A disastrous fire" on page 34 for more details about the 1895 fire.
[6] The resignation of President Alexander was part of the merger agreement with Pittsburgh Female College calling for its president, N.H. Holmes, to become President of the combined institutions.

W. J. Alexander, President
(1894–1896). (Beaver Area
Historical Museum)

Nicholas H. Holmes, President
(1896–1898). (Beaver Area
Historical Museum)

EXCUSE CARD.

Beaver, Pa., *April 14, 1896.*

Miss *Wittish* is excused

for absence on *4 — 16 & 13; — 14 — C.H. 1896,*

from *All.*

W. J. Alexander,

ave Instructors endorse, and return to Office.

Absence excuse card for
Miss Wittish, April 14, 1896.
(Arcadia University Archives)

Arthur Staples, President (1898–1907). (Beaver Area Historical Museum)

George D. Crissman, President (1907–1909). (Arcadia University Archives)

William W. Foster, President (1909–1910). (Arcadia University Archives)

President Staples and the 1901 college body in corridor of College Hall. (Beaver Area Historical Museum)

Pittsburgh Female College circa 1890. (Library and Archives Division, Historical Society of Western Pennsylvania, Pittsburgh, Pa.)

also under the Pittsburgh Conference [of the Church]. A merger had been proposed by Beaver College some years earlier, but the trustees of the Pittsburgh institution had not agreed to it, and since then had spent the years in a fruitless attempt to find a permanent home for their institution after their own disastrous fire. Beaver College was very much in debt and a pooling of resources was thought the best solution of their respective problems. Many students of the Pittsburgh college continued as boarding students at Beaver. Transference of some of their teachers was, of course, of advantage to them. Dormitory facilities being not as yet available for the transferring students, temporary rooms for them were secured in homes of selected citizens. The new buildings at Beaver, one for classes and assemblies and the other a girls' dormitory, were connected by a covered bridge. Upon the completion of the dormitory, the president and his wife and five of the lady teachers lived in this dormitory, which boasted washrooms on each floor with hot and cold water. Young men were housed in suitable homes and boarding clubs in the town.

At this time Beaver College received a number of Monongahela Coal and Coke bonds from the Pittsburgh Female College, and in 1899 the trustees of this institution gave Beaver College $25,000 of the sum realized from the sale of their old college property in Pittsburgh. With the new buildings at Beaver and the enrollment increased by the Pittsburgh Female

College girls, who entered into the activities of their new Alma Mater enthusiastically, the spirit of Beaver College and Musical Institute gave promise of a greater future as the turn of the century approached.

Although Beaver received its charter as a college in 1872, for some reason it was not until 1903 that the University Senate of the Methodist Episcopal Church changed its classification from seminary to college.[7] The last charter change in title [until the advent of Arcadia University] was made in 1907 when the name Beaver College and Musical Institute was simplified to Beaver College. At the same time the enrollment was limited to women.

Entrance to the freshman class of the college of liberal arts was by one of three methods: examinations covering the entrance subjects (English, Latin, history, mathematics, Greek, German or French, natural science or a third foreign language), by certificate or diploma from high schools and academies of approved grade, and by diploma from the preparatory department of Beaver College . . . .

In 1909, in addition to the departments in liberal arts, the institution included the academy or college preparatory department and schools of music and

continued on page 38

[7] The University Senate was the accrediting body of the Methodist Episcopal Church. Formed in 1892, it first applied its standards for college status to the various educational institutions of the Church in 1894. Up until 1903, the Annual Report of the Church's Board of Education listed Beaver College as a female seminary. Even though Beaver College was chartered as a college by the State, it did not meet the accrediting standards of the University Senate until that year.

Beaver College in 1894 before the fire. (Beaver Area Historical Museum)

A DISASTROUS FIRE

"College Building Destroyed! The Beaver College and Musical Institute Goes Up in Flames and Smoke—The Building Totally Destroyed But Most of Its Contents Saved," blared the headlines of *The Weekly Star of* Beaver, Pa. "A Disastrous Fire! Beaver College Destroyed by Fire Saturday Morning," stated the town's *Argus and Radical*. The conflagration occurred on Saturday, February 23, 1895.

The February 28, 1895 weekly edition of the *Argus and Radical* reported, "About half past six o'clock Saturday morning the slumbering citizens of Beaver were alarmed by the cry of fire. Soon the fire alarm sounded and people began to run towards Beaver College where the fire was located. The smoke was pouring out the roof at the tower in the rear, and the fire was located in the attic, probably in the old roof which had been left and was covered over with slate."

The Weekly Star for February 28, 1895 added the following details:

The discovery was first made by someone passing up College Avenue, who notified Janitor Pollard. The latter at once awoke Prof. Pollock and a student named Kell, who roomed in the building. The two quickly passed from room to room and aroused the sleeping students notifying them to gather up their personal effects and vacate their rooms. In a short time all the students were safe on the outside with their luggage.

The fire first started in the attic and is supposed to have been caused from burning soot in one of the flues connected with the furnace operating the heaters. While but little headway was made by the flames at first there was no way of extinguishing them owing to the scarcity of water. The plug on the corner was found frozen up and not a particle of water could be obtained. The hose companies of New Brighton and Beaver Falls went to assist in subduing the fire, but like the Beaver fire department, which was early on the ground, were helpless for lack of water.

It was very soon apparent that the building could not be saved and all hands went to work carrying out the contents. In this the willing helpers were remarkably successful. Of the nine fine and costly pianos in the building seven were carried out, though some were more or less damaged. The grand, a very valuable instrument, had one of its legs broken in the removal. A large amount of other moveable property was saved, though a portion of the most valuable was lost. Among the latter was a splendid telescope valued at $5,000.

Beaver College fire
in 1895. (Beaver Area
Historical Museum)

The ruins of the College
immediately after the fire.
(Beaver Area Historical Museum)

The *Argus and Radical* lamented the loss of the College's memorial windows. It complained, "Some of them might have been [saved] had timely and well directed efforts been made, but what is everybody's business is nobody's. The excitement and short time in which anything could be done, rendered it impossible to do what otherwise might have been accomplished."

In all, the loss was estimated at over $45,000. In 2002 dollars, the loss would be equivalent to $1,000,000. The building was insured for only $20,000 and the furnishings and equipment for $5,000. Most of the furnishings and carpeting were new. The entire college building had been refurnished and renovated only the summer before. To add insult to injury, the *Argus and Radical* reported, the evening after the fire, thieves tried to break into the College's laundry where the things salvaged from the college building were stored. Mr. James Pollard, the janitor, was sleeping there and frightened them away.

Such fires were not infrequent in those days and often had devastating effects. Beaver College's sister school, Pittsburgh Female College, never recovered from a similar fire in 1891, and the two institutions eventually merged. Beaver College was justly proud of the fact that not a day of classes was missed as a result of the conflagration. Classes were relocated to local churches and public schools and took place as scheduled Monday morning. Students were housed with local families and in a nearby hotel, the Beaver House. Extracurricular events and athletic events continued. The Board of Trustees met the very afternoon of the fire and resolved that the College would continue and the building be rebuilt. They promised "A new building, more beautiful, more convenient will spring from the ashes of the old." A wealthy resident, Mr. L. Leonard, offered to give $2,000 toward the new building. The April 11, 1895 *Argus and Radical* reported on the Board's plans for a new building to be erected on the old site. The estimated cost of the building was $20,000, the amount of the insurance. On May 13, 1895, the contract for the new building was awarded to local contractors Tallon and Farr. By August 22, 1895, the walls of the new building were completed and work on the roof begun. The new building was dedicated on December 3, 1895, just ten months after the College was burned to the ground. A new dormitory was built and occupied two years later in 1897. *Samuel M. Cameron*

Sources
Argus and Radical, February 28, 1895.
Argus and Radical, April 11, 1895.
Minutes of the Board of Trustees of Beaver College.
The Weekly Star, February 28, 1895.

Art studio in the new
College Hall. (Beaver Area
Historical Museum)

Biology Laboratory in College
Hall. (Photo by Brown,
Beaver, Pa.; Beaver Area
Historical Museum)

Dr. Chevalier Giuseppe Ferrata,
Director of the Musical
Department (1903–1910).
(Beaver Area Historical Museum)

oratory, and the college granted the degrees of A.B., B.O., B.Mus., and M.Mus. After 1911 a modern language might be substituted for the one year of classics before prescribed. In 1919, one hundred and twenty semester hours were required for the degree of Bachelor of Arts or Bachelor of Science. Other degrees offered were Master of Arts, Master of Science, Bachelor of Music, Bachelor of Oratory, and Bachelor of Science in Home Economics.

Throughout the first quarter of this century Beaver College was known most significantly for its outstanding music department, and its students and graduates in this field made up much the largest group. Some graduates continued their studies at their Alma Mater for the Master's Degree. Reminiscences of two of the graduates of 1912 revealed that nothing daunted the zeal of music students, who, practicing on twelve pianos and an organ, all concentrated at the back of the chapel, or vocalizing in the same place, triumphed over the dissonance of bedlam to provide in concerts feasts of fine music, supported enthusiastically not only by the students but also by the citizens of Beaver and the far reaches of the Ohio valley. Senior recitals in piano, voice, and violin especially were musts for lovers of Bach, Mozart, Beethoven, and Brahms. No student practiced fewer than four hours a day on the piano alone, and teachers added to the instruction they gave in the two private lessons a week frequent supervision of parts of the practice sessions.

Music continued to dominate extracurricular activities too. In 1902 the Liszt musical club was organized "for the studying of eminent composers, the rendition of musical programs, the cultivation and development of the musical taste of the community, and the securing of such artists as may be determined by the club." The Chaminade Club,[8] consisting of college girls, gave from six to ten concerts a year, and the Monday Musical, a mixed chorus of sixty voices composed of representative singers of the Beaver valley and conducted by the director of the voice department, was open to college students of the upper grades.

The aim of the college continued to be to foster the highest type of Christian manhood and womanhood, its succeeding administrations recognizing that no education is complete without moral and religious development. At the turn of the century devotional exercises were held in the chapel each morning at nine o'clock. By 1919 chapel exercises, conducted on Tuesday (there were no classes on Monday), Wednesday, Thursday, Friday, and Saturday mornings at 10 o'clock, provided worship, instruction, and inspiration as well as entertainment. All students were required to attend Sunday morning worship at the church of their choice, and a Y.W.C.A. chapter, organized about 1906, was active.

[8] Most likely named after Cecile Chaminade (b. Paris, August 1857, d. April 13, 1944), a French female composer popular around the turn of the 20th century.

Chaminade Club.
(Arcadia University Archives)

The Chapel in College Hall
with pipe organ circa 1907.
(Arcadia University Archives)

Mrs. Sarah B. Cochran, Beaver
College benefactor. (Beaver
Area Historical Museum)

Dr. Alexander W. Crawford,
Dean of the College
(1903–1906). (Beaver Area
Historical Museum)

Dr. LeRoy Weller, Professor
(1907–1910), Dean of
the College (1909–1910),
President (1910–1917).
(Arcadia University Archives)

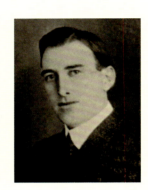

THE CLARISSA COCHRAN MEMORIAL CHAIR OF ENGLISH AND PHILOSOPHY

On November 7, 1902, President Arthur Staples told the Board of Trustees that Mrs. Sarah B. Cochran had promised $30,000 ($462,000 in 2002 dollars) to endow the "Clarissa Cochran Memorial Chair of English and Philosophy." While the College records contain no mention of Clarissa, two other Cochran children attended the institution: William G. who studied in the Commercial Department during the academic year 1898–1899, and Katherine who studied in the Music Department in 1899–1900. By 1905, Mrs. Cochran had fulfilled her pledge. The money was invested in bank certificates and produced an annual income of 5.4% ($1,620). As the occupant of the Chair was paid $1,300, the endowment should have enjoyed some growth over time.

The first recipient of the endowed Chair was Wilber G. Compher, Ph.D., Dean of the College and Professor of English and Philosophy. He died during the summer of 1903, and Dr. Alexander W. Crawford, newly recruited, was appointed to the Chair and became Dean of the College. Dr. Crawford came to Beaver College from Ursinus College where he had been Professor of Philosophy and Psychology. One of the first things he did after arriving at Beaver College was to set up an experimental psychology laboratory. He stayed only two years and was succeeded as occupant of the Chair by the Reverend LeRoy Weller, for whom the name of the Chair was changed to read "Clarissa Cochran Memorial Chair of Greek and Philosophy," reflecting his teaching assignments. Dr. Weller continued to hold the Chair when he became Dean of the College in 1909 and President in 1910 upon the resignation of President William W. Foster. The 1911 College Catalog indicates another change in name of the endowed Chair to the "Clarissa Cochran Memorial Chair of Philosophy and Psychology," which reflects Dr. Weller's academic training, but does not list him, or anyone else, as occupant.

In February 1911, $6,570 of the College's outstanding loans were called unexpectedly and, without any financial reserves and everything mortgaged, it faced an acute financial crisis. The April 1911 minutes of the Board of Trustees indicate that Mrs. Cochran gave her consent that the money remaining in the endowment be used to liquidate the College's debt. Following 1911, College catalogs make no mention of the endowed chair.

It was not until 1996, eighty-five years later, that the College again had endowed chairs. In that year, The Stacy Anne Vitteta '82 Professorship in the natural sciences, and The Frank and Evelyn Steinbrucker '43 Endowed Chair in the social sciences were established. *Samuel M. Cameron*

Sources
Bulletins (Catalogs) of Beaver College, 1898–1911
Minutes of the Beaver College Board of Trustees, 1902–1911

Student Life in the Early Twentieth Century

Although bowling "to get necessary exercise in bad weather" had been enjoyed at Beaver since 1886 and the Trustees' Minutes of 1894 record authorization and purchase by the president of a tennis set for use by the students (total cost $9.50), and although there are records of petitions by the men and boys to be allowed some time for use of the gymnasium, seemingly here at least a woman's world, it was not until 1898–1899 that a college catalogue devoted a section to athletics, which, it states, "although not holding as prominent a place as at some colleges have not been entirely neglected." In *The Beaver*, another creditable all-college monthly news-magazine, begun in 1899, we read of basketball and football teams and of tennis for young ladies, of a bowling alley and a croquet ground. We also learn of a "large, well equipped gymnasium" (without mention of the hazard of an iron pole in the center) open for the free use of all students at periods assigned to them, with regular classes conducted by the teachers of physical education.

Although *The Beaver* records such intercollegiate successes as those in baseball in 1904 against Geneva, Rochester Business College, Mt. Union College, and Washington and Jefferson, inter-school and inter-collegiate games generally proved Beaver students' greater aptitude for the classics, and the most hoped for by the girls of Beaver in a game with Geneva College was that they "be not white washed" . . . .

College life in the second decade of the new century continued, as with the Taylors, family style with the women faculty members residing at college and acting as hostesses and chaperones. Social graces were taught at table, and further practiced at receptions and teas. Rules were strict but exercised with reason by the Preceptress. Resident students, women only after the charter change of 1907, were not allowed off campus except between 3:30 and 5:00 p.m. unless accompanied by a senior or a teacher. All dates were chaperoned and those enjoyed nearby terminated not later than 9:30 p.m. Dancing, except by girls with each other, and smoking were forbidden. On occasion, however, the social hall was the scene of "conversations" with young men, for which programs were often provided, each conversation of the evening being limited to five minutes.

In these "old fashioned" days there was a true quiet hour, according to alumnae. From 9:00 to 10:00 p.m. and lights-out, students might relax from their studies with such diversions as chafing dish spreads. Even later than that ultimate hour daring ones sometimes arranged these bed-time snacks by candlelight under the canopy of a concealing umbrella. Food was good but not infallible and during this period of the teens when shrimp salad was a regular Saturday night occurrence, a whole table was known to rise and walk to Rochester [a nearby town across the Beaver River] for more varied fare. Oddly and for no apparent

Scenes from the Women's Residence Hall. (Beaver Area Historical Museum)

The parlor.

A student room.

The dining room.

reason, mince pie was served only once a year . . . . At commencement seniors gathered hundreds of marbles and at two or three a.m. threw them down the wooden, uncarpeted stairs.

Around the turn of the century, the active literary societies succumbed, perhaps to the rapidly shifting academic emphasis, but the Owlet and Parthenon societies were resuscitated in 1906, and such clubs as the Reviewers and Chaminade flourished. As time went on a student council functioned and the honor system prevailed in residence and home economics halls . . . .

For a good many years before the removal to Jenkintown, Beaver College had been struggling along under the hazardous necessity of making ends meet on practically nothing but student fees. Charges for room and board varied from $325 to $450, depending on accommodations, and in 1921 tuition was $100. But students were scarce, very scarce in spite of appeals to all age levels from preparatory to graduate school and offerings in liberal arts, music, fine arts, expression, and public school music. In 1919 there were two graduate students, sixteen regular undergraduates in liberal arts, eighty-two in music, eighteen in fine arts, twenty-two in expression, twenty-two listed as college specials, and fifteen in the academy.

But testified to both by those who were students then and indicated by more exacting admission requirements and graduation standards, the ideal of an institution strong academically was upheld staunchly in spite of the

fiscal handwriting on the wall. Even then, honor graduates of high school classes were especially sought and won by offers of scholarships.

During the tenure of President William Thoburn, 1921–1923, a last attempt was made to relieve the institution of its financial handicap. At this time when Methodist colleges everywhere were raising money it was decided to put on a drive for capital funds for removal to a new site on a hill at the edge of town and for an endowment fund. The Pittsburgh Conference endorsed the drive and engaged an official church money-raising organization to conduct the "Forward Look" campaign for Beaver . . . .[9]

With expenses piling up and very little coming in The Pittsburgh Conference decided to terminate the drive. In 1923 The Conference of the Methodist Church refused to recognize Beaver as a college for future contributions.[10] In this critical time a new president, Lynn H. Harris, was called in to raise funds. Among those who had faith in the survival of the college were four trustees, Mr. Winfield S. Moore, Mr. Homer P. Hartley, Mr. Harry B. Richardson, and Mr. Robert W. Darragh.

[9] See the essay "Good Intentions Gone Awry" on page 46 for a detailed account of this disastrous fundraising campaign.

[10] Higgins and Sturgeon report this event incorrectly. The College lost its accreditation by the Methodist University Senate in 1923; the Senate no longer recognized Beaver College as an institution qualified to issue a Bachelor's degree. The Pittsburgh Conference threatened to cut off contributions to the College, but continued to provide some funding while the institution attempted to solve its financial dilemma. See the essay "Good Intentions Gone Awry" for more details about these decisions.

Student production of "As You Like It" circa 1910. (Arcadia University Archives)

The last meeting of alumnae
in Beaver, Pa., June 1925. The
group is posed on the porch
stairs in front of the Women's
Residence of the College.
(Beaver College Archives)

From here and there over the next two years the new president picked up enough in driblets to pay running expenses, the interest on the notes, and to somewhat reduce the indebtedness. Meanwhile, President Harris, convinced the only living solution was relocation, corresponded with a number of prospects. Finally, Dr. Matthew Reaser, head of the Beechwood School in Jenkintown, was attracted by the unusually advantageous charter of Beaver College.[11] With the control remaining in the hands of the Board of Trustees, attorneys for the College drew up papers which provided that the college purchase Beechwood School for the sum of $220,000 of which a small part was lent by the Beechwood School and the remainder taken care of by a . . . mortgage. Next, the property in Beaver, consisting of a block of city real estate with a house and two buildings on it, was sold to the town of Beaver for school purposes.

[11] See the essay "The Pot at the End of the Rainbow" on page 86 for more details about the factors entering into the decision to merge the two institutions.

The demolition of Beaver Senior High School (formerly College Hall) in 1980. (Photo by Rudy Schunk, *Beaver County Times*, Beaver, Pa.)

GOOD INTENTIONS GONE AWRY

AN ESSAY

Samuel M. Cameron

Dr. Horace B. Haskell,
President (1917–1919).
(Reproduced with permission
from the United Methodist
Church Archives–GCAH)

Franklin Hamilton, Bishop of
the Methodist Episcopal Church.
(Reproduced with permission
from the Drew University
Library Methodist Collection)

In 1917, the Trustees of Beaver College under the leadership of new College President Horace B. Haskell, and with the support and urging of the Pittsburgh Conference of the Episcopal Methodist Church, began a noble effort to upgrade Beaver College into a leading women's college. The report of the Education Committee to the Pittsburgh Conference's annual meeting in October 1917 stated, "With the coming of President Horace B. Haskell to Beaver College, a new and better day is dawning upon that institution. It is the only educational institution of the church within the borders of our Conference . . . . This opens the field for a campaign of $1,000,000 [$14,000,000 in 2002 dollars] for the purpose of equipment and endowment. Should we not as a Conference . . . undertake to make Beaver College one of the best colleges for women in America?" This noble goal was to lead, six years later, to financial disaster, the demise of the College in Beaver, Pennsylvania, and its move east to Jenkintown.

When Dr. Haskell assumed office, the College was under pressure from several directions. The number of students was steadily shrinking; tuition, room and board were insufficient to pay operating expenses. The institution was heavily in debt; its real estate was fully mortgaged and its small endowment used as collateral for loans used to pay current expenses. Finally, the University Senate, the accrediting arm of the Episcopal Methodist Church's Board of Education, required the College to improve its financial situation, raise $200,000 for endowment, increase its faculty, and improve and enlarge its physical plant in order to continue to have the Senate's approval as an institution granting the bachelor's degree.

Members of the College's Board of Trustees discussed the need for a fundraising effort, and in May 1917, even before Dr. Haskell became president, a campaign was agreed upon with a final goal of $500,000 and an initial phase target of $250,000. Resident Bishop Hamilton was to serve as Chair of the campaign.

However, events transpired to delay the implementation of a drive to meet this modest and probably achievable goal. Bishop Hamilton, a strong supporter of the concept of a "Greater Beaver College," died May 5, 1918, and was succeeded by Franklin J. McConnell. When the Board again discussed the fundraising campaign in late 1918, the goal was increased to $1,000,000. Concrete plans for the fund drive, however, were delayed.

In part, the delay can be attributed to explorations of a possible merger with Pennsylvania College for Women (later Chatham College). Both colleges had pressing financial concerns and it was hoped that the proposed merger would result in a stronger, more secure entity. The Beaver Trustees wanted the institution to be located in Beaver and had secured options on land for such a purpose, while the Pennsylvania College for Women wanted to remain in Pittsburgh. Negotiations floundered on this difference. Furthermore, the Beaver College Club, an alumni organization, went on record favoring a Greater Beaver College, but opposing the merger with Pennsylvania College for Women.

Appleton Bash, a Trustee of Beaver College and a member of the Methodist Church's Commission on Women's College, at the October 1921 Annual Meeting of the Pittsburgh Conference, called for the dissolution of that commission and the formation of a smaller committee that, in consultation with the newly appointed Beaver College President J. M. Thoburn, Jr., would have "full power to determine the future program for college work within the Pittsburgh Conference."

This "Committee of Nine" would "have authority to continue Beaver College at Beaver, Pennsylvania, as an institution of college grade provided the city of Beaver and vicinity give a site satisfactory to the Committee and in addition shall give a sum satisfactory to the Committee for the erection of new buildings; and in event of the failure of the city of Beaver and vicinity to comply with these conditions then the Committee may provide for the re-organization of Beaver College as a secondary school for girls." The Committee of Nine would have one year to report on the success or failure of the proposed plan. The Conference's adoption of Bash's motion marked the end of the negotiations for merger of the two colleges and the beginning of a disastrous capital campaign.

On February 7, 1922, the Board of Trustees met to consider a report from the Committee of Nine and to hear the advice of Dr. John Hancher, fundraiser for the Methodist Episcopal Church. The Committee of Nine recommended that a campaign to secure $250,000 from Beaver, Pennsylvania, and vicinity to buy a site and erect new buildings should be conducted simultaneously with a larger campaign to secure the first unit of $1,000,000. Dr. Hancher urged the Board to accept the Committee of Nine's report, but suggested that they increase the initial goal of the campaign to $1,500,000 with a final goal of $3,000,000. The Board accepted Dr. Hancher's advice and requested the help of the Methodist Episcopal Church to raise money to build and endow the new facility. The original modest proposal for raising $500,000 made five years earlier had now multiplied to what would prove to be an unrealistic total of $3,000,000.

At a meeting of the Board of Trustees on September 11, 1922, the Committee of Nine recommended that Beaver College proceed with the fundraising drive. President Thoburn reported that certain local trustees and citizens of Beaver had secured an option on forty-five acres of land that would cost $32,000. This site was on a hill overlooking the city of Beaver

Rev. Appleton Bash, Associate President of the College (1923–1924) and member of the Board of Trustees. (Beaver Area Historical Museum)

Dr. James M. Thoburn, Jr., President (1921–1923). (Reproduced with permission from the United Methodist Church Archives–GCAH)

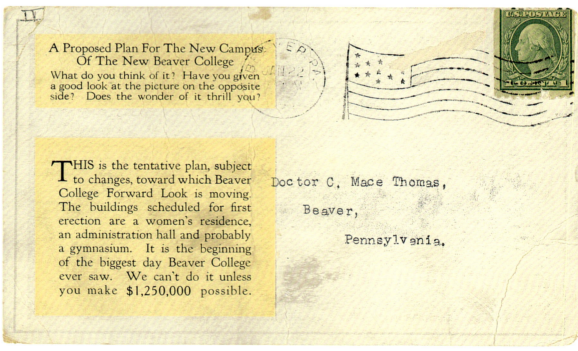

A Proposed Plan For The New Campus
Of The New Beaver College
What do you think of it? Have you given
a good look at the picture on the opposite
side? Does the wonder of it thrill you?

THIS is the tentative plan, subject
to changes, toward which Beaver
College Forward Look is moving.
The buildings scheduled for first
erection are a women's residence,
an administration hall and probably
a gymnasium. It is the beginning
of the biggest day Beaver College
ever saw. We can't do it unless
you make $1,250,000 possible.

Doctor C. Mace Thomas,

Beaver,

Pennsylvania.

The front and back of a postcard used as a promotional device during
the 1923 Forward Look fundraising campaign. The front shows a
drawing of the proposed new campus of Beaver College on Windy
Ghoul, a hill overlooking Beaver, Pa. The back solicits donations
to the campaign. The card is addressed to C. Mace Thomas who
was Dean of the College at the time. (Arcadia University Archives)

called "Windy Ghoul." On the strength of these two encouraging reports, the Trustees unanimously voted to adopt the report of the Committee of Nine and to proceed with the campaign, which they named the Forward Look Drive.

On September 18, 1922, the trustees met to consider means of financing the campaign. They decided that the College should first secure guarantors or endorsers to finance the drive before incurring any other binding obligations. The Board also reconsidered its action at the previous meeting and lowered the goal for the initial stage of the campaign to $1,250,000, to be "validated" at $1,000,000, i.e., pledges to the Forward Look Drive need not be paid unless $1,000,000 was raised. Ultimately, this proviso was the undoing of the campaign, which never came close to raising $1,000,000.

At the annual meeting of the Pittsburgh Conference in October 1922, the Committee on Beaver College (the former Committee of Nine) reported that it had decided to continue Beaver College and that the College "had met every requirement imposed and [was] instituting a forward movement for the raising of a fund of $1,250,000 to develop it into a high-grade standard college for women." The Conference's Committee on Education presented its report stating that the campaign "should challenge the members and constituents of the Pittsburgh Conference to a ready and generous response . . . . And to this movement we pledge our loyal and unfailing co-operation and support." The Education Committee's report was adopted unanimously, followed by a standing ovation.

Meeting on December 11, 1922, the Board of Trustees heard a report from Dr. John W. McDougal, the Pittsburgh Conference's field manager for the Campaign, on the various preparations that had been made. He stated that the Campaign was to be launched January 7, 1923, and closed February 28, 1923. The Church had used such brief, intense campaigns successfully in prior college fundraising efforts. The actual launch date, according to local newspapers was Sunday, January 14, 1923, when the ministers in all of the churches throughout the Pittsburgh Conference urged their members to aid the campaign.

The newspapers predicted great success for the campaign, but such was not to be. A sign that not all was well was the appearance of a special letter sent by Edward W. Chellin, Chairman of the Forward Look Drive, and addressed to "You Whose Earnest Cooperation Beaver College Forward Look Craves, Solicits And Must Have." It stated, "This evening of January twenty six, we are at the place where it would be easy for Beaver College to fail. Unless we set Beaver Valley and constituent regions on fire with enthusiasm, our $1,250,000 will be in jeopardy." By January 29, 1923, the Beaver area had raised only $105,000 including money to purchase the Windy Ghoul site. On February 8, 1923, the weekly *Pittsburgh Christian Advocate* ran a special article urging its readers, primarily members of the Pittsburgh Conference, to support the campaign.

On February 15, 1923, Reverend Jacob S. Payton, President of the College's Board of Trustees, called a special meeting of the Board. The minutes report, "Remarks by

BEAVER COLLEGE FOR WOMEN

BEAVER, PENNSYLVANIA

$1,250,000.00

For Enlargement and Endowment

One of the oldest Colleges exclusively for Women about to become the newest College in equipment, buildings and outlook.

A College of Liberal Arts

Degrees, Diplomas and Certificates
ALSO GIVEN IN
Music, Art, Expression and Home Economics

For Catalogue and Other Information Address
PRESIDENT J. M. THOBURN, JR., Beaver, Pa.

An advertisement for the ill-fated Forward Look Drive. (Arcadia University Archives)

Dr. Hancher showed the seriousness of the situation relative to the Forward Look and he was followed by Dr. McDougal who spoke of the general apathy of the people . . . and by Mr. Conant, that three local chairmen had done practically nothing, and that fourteen local Methodist Episcopal churches had taken negative action and that the city of Pittsburgh had no effective organization." After vigorous debate over continuing or stopping the campaign, the consensus was to continue the campaign and Bishop McConnell was "requested to call together the Pittsburgh Conference, to consider the Beaver College Drive situation."

Four days later, the Conference met in special session. After extensive discussion, Bishop McConnell stated two alternatives to be voted upon: continuing the campaign until February 28 or stopping the campaign at once, but supporting a special collection for the benefit of the guarantors of the campaign. The special session voted to end the campaign by a vote of 90 to 28. Both the *Beaver Falls Tribune* and Beaver's *The Daily Times* interpreted the resolution of the special session as protecting the guarantors against loss. The *Beaver Falls Tribune*, reporting the next day on the decision to close the campaign, said that only $250,000 had been pledged. As $1,000,000 in pledges was needed to validate any pledge, no money was actually raised by the campaign.

Franklin J. McConnell,
Bishop of the Methodist
Episcopal Church.
(Reproduced with permission
from the Drew University
Library Methodist Collection)

The Trustees of the College, however, were reluctant to accept the decision of the special session of the Pittsburgh Conference. At a regularly scheduled meeting on March 5, 1923, Dr. Bash closely questioned Dr. Hancher whether in his opinion, in light of the fact that some of his workers were confident that $100,000 to $150,000 in additional subscriptions would have been obtained if the campaign had not been ended by the special session of the Conference, the Board had a right to proceed with the Forward Look Drive. Dr. Hancher replied that the Pittsburgh Conference would certainly not hold the Board guilty if they succeeded in raising funds and that, if the Conference approved, he would furnish, at the latter's expense, two workers to help in this endeavor. A motion was made and seconded to request Dr. Hancher to make an additional appeal for a scaled down Forward Look Drive of $500,000 to $600,000. The next day, *The Daily News* headlines stated, "Trustees decide college campaign should continue. Beaver will endeavor to raise $600,000."

At the March 22, 1923 Board meeting, Dr. Bash presented the reply of the Committee of Nine to the College's request for approval to reopen the campaign. The Committee felt that it had no authority to reverse the decision of the special session of the Pittsburgh Conference, but that the Trustees of the College had the right to make any decision they wanted as long as they did not represent it as being endorsed by the Conference. After discussion, the Trustees voted, 6 in favor, 2 against, and 4 abstaining, to resume the drive with subscriptions being validated once $500,000 was raised.

Bishop McConnell and several campaign workers attended the April Board of Trustees meeting. The workers reported that $77,000 in pledges had been obtained from the original subscribers to the campaign. This amount was considerably less then the $250,000 previously subscribed. Dr. Payton, President of the Board of Trustees, voiced his belief that "Beaver College could not well continue longer under present conditions." A motion that the meeting be adjourned and the discussion of continuing the College be taken up at a session the following week was approved.

At that next meeting, the Board was rocked by a succession of negative reports. College President Thoburn stated that he felt he should retire from the presidency. Following Thoburn's announcement, Dr. Payton stated that the question before the Board was, "Shall we continue Beaver College." Mr. Moore moved, seconded by Mr. Darragh, that Beaver College should be continued. Dr. Bash then read a letter from Dr. A. W. Harris of the Educational Board of the Episcopal Methodist Church stating that the Board "could not continue to recognize Beaver College as a College." Dr. Payton read a letter from Bishop McConnell stating, "I greatly fear that some of the Beaver College trustees are supporting the proposition to continue the work of the College under a misunderstanding. There is no assurance that the College will continue to receive the Educational Collection [the annual Church appropriation] in the future . . . . I have grave doubts as to whether either the Conference or the Board will long continue to vote Educational funds to Beaver."

A general discussion of the fate of the College then followed. Some spoke in favor of the College becoming a secondary school, others argued in favor of continuing as a college. Dr. Bash offered a substitute to the motion that the College should continue. He moved, "It is the sentiment of this Board that Beaver College shall continue its work of education with the understanding that we will graduate any student who is now matriculated in the school with proper scholastic degree if earned by June 1924, but that we will not accept any student for any course of study with assurance to confer college degrees that lead beyond the standard of work usually required by the Junior College. It is understood that this action is to be binding until June 1924 at which time, or before, such date the Board will determine the future policy." The substitute motion carried 10 to 2 with 7 trustees abstaining. Bash's compromise allowed the College to continue to explore ways to survive as an institution of higher education.

At the Board's regular meeting in June, President Thoburn officially offered his resignation to take effect at the annual meeting of the Pittsburgh Conference in October. Dr. Thoburn's resignation was accepted and a search committee was appointed to find a new president. New trustees were elected, and the Board reorganized with those who favored continuation of the College serving as officers.

The newly constituted Board met on June 25, 1923, and discussion of the continuance of the College was resumed with no concrete decisions being made. The Finance Committee was authorized to issue notes of the College in payment of expenses incurred by Forward Look to any creditors that would accept them. At its August 2, 1923, meeting, the Search Committee recommended and the Board approved Lynn H. Harris, Ph.D., as the next President.

At its annual meeting in October 1923, the Pittsburgh Conference spent most of a day on the pressing and embarrassing issue of Beaver College. Appleton Bash presented a set of recommendations from the Committee of Nine, including one endorsing the idea that the guarantors of the expenses of Forward Look be compensated. The Committee also recommended that the Conference request the Trustees of Beaver College "meet the conditions prescribed by the Church for the recognition of schools of college grade or failing to meet this requirement of the Church they reorganize the school so that it can be recognized as a school of secondary grade or a junior college. Further the Committee recommends that if the above conditions are not met by the Trustees of Beaver College by October 1, 1924, the Conference take such action at that time as they deem proper in the case." All of the above recommendations were approved by the Conference. In addition, the Committee had recommended that the Educational Committee of the Conference continue funding of the College on the same level as the previous year. After some discussion, a compromise, but generous, amount of the current year's Education Collection of the Pittsburgh Conference was awarded to Beaver College.

Dr. Lynn H. Harris,
President (1923–1928).
(Arcadia University Archives)

At its December 17, 1923, meeting, the Beaver College Board of Trustees considered ways to raise funds to compensate the guarantors of the Forward Look Drive, the continuance of the College as a college or secondary school, and the need for $2,400 to meet current expenses. Approximately $6,000 was still owed on Forward Look over and above the amounts owed the guarantors. At a Board meeting in January 1924 with Bishop McConnell and the Committee of Nine, President Harris reported that the amount now due the guarantors was $48,650. Bishop McConnell was requested to send a letter to the ministers of the Pittsburgh Conference asking that they have an offering to reimburse the guarantors of the Forward Look Drive for Beaver College, and that his District Superintendents also follow up on his letter with a letter to each pastor in their district setting an amount each Church was to raise.

At the annual meeting of the Pittsburgh Conference held in October 1924, the Education Committee made positive comments on Beaver College stating, "We commend it to our people who desire a school of wholesome and cultured Christian influences for the education of their daughters." The only business item relating to Beaver College concerned the matter of reimbursing the guarantors. A motion was introduced that a Committee of Five be appointed to see to raising the money pledged by the Conference. The motion was amended by a close vote to add, "that every pastor pledges his personal honor to present the matter to his people and use his influence to secure this money within sixty days." The final motion carried by a large majority.

Despite such strong sentiments and positive intentions, minuscule funds were raised. The appeal following the close of the Campaign by the special session of the Conference in February 1923 raised $2,093.75 from twenty churches, 70% of which was contributed by the Beaver church and one other. Subsequent appeals, including the one appealing to the ministers' honor, raised an additional $4,000. Thus, the Pittsburgh Conference, consisting of over 200 Churches in one of the wealthiest areas in the nation, raised a total of only $6,093.75 in two years to pay the expenses of a capital campaign that it had led the College into mounting.

On December 29, 1924, Dr. Matthew H. Reaser, President of the Beechwood School in Jenkintown, Pennsylvania, offered a plan to improve Beaver College's financial situation by merging it with the Beechwood School (a junior college) in suburban Philadelphia.

Dr. Reaser proposed that he loan Beaver College $20,000 and that the real property of the College be sold to raise an additional $75,000, the total of $95,000 to be used to pay Beaver's debts. The College would then be in a position to purchase or lease the land, buildings, equipment and furnishings of the Jenkintown school. The offer was dependent on two provisos: that the guarantors of the Forward Look Drive release their claim against Beaver College at 60% of the amount outstanding and that the charter of the College be amended to allow for a smaller Board of Trustees and for the purchase, lease, or operation of the Beechwood School. At a meeting held on February 9, 1925, College President Harris reported that the guarantors had agreed to accept 60% of what they had advanced the College. He then presented a proposed agreement providing for the merger of Beaver College and the Beechwood School, which was approved on February 17, 1925.

Eventually, the Beaver College property was sold to the Beaver School Board and became its high school. Beaver College, no longer a Methodist institution, moved to Jenkintown, still under heavy debt. A report on the history of the educational efforts of the Pittsburgh Conference by William L. Wilkenson published in the minutes of the October 1925 Annual Conference stated, "Several months ago it was announced that the college had 'made disposal of its property and would cease to operate in Beaver with the coming commencement' and that 'with the opening of the college year it would operate in its new location at Jenkintown, Pa.,' adding that 'with this action the affiliation of Beaver College with the Methodist Episcopal Church is severed.' Some folks will always feel that the Pittsburgh Conference as a whole has had the interests of Beaver College at heart. Some folks, it is said, are just as confident that the Conference was not whole-heartedly loyal to the college. All will doubtless agree on one point, namely, that the Conference will heave a long and perhaps repeated sigh of relief that it will no longer need to face a situation which has seemed 'impossible.' Most of the members of the Conference have a sincere hope that the college may have large success in its new location."

Dr. Matthew H. Reaser, President of Beechwood School. (Arcadia University Archives)

Sources

Beaver Falls Tribune, Beaver Falls, Pa.

Letter from Edward W. Crellin, Beaver, Pa., to "You Whose Earnest Cooperation Beaver College Forward Look Craves, Solicits And Must Have," January 26, 1923.

Minutes of the Annual Meeting of the Pittsburgh Conference of the Episcopal Methodist Church.

Minutes of the Beaver College Board of Trustees.

Pittsburgh Christian Advocate, Pittsburgh, Pa.

The Daily News, Beaver, Pa.

BEAVER COLLEGE IN BEAVER, PA.

A PHOTO ESSAY

College Hall was dedicated in December 1895, the Women's Residence Hall (on the right) in 1897. (Beaver Area Historical Museum)

Corridor and stairs in the Women's Residence Hall, circa 1908. (Arcadia University Archives)

Room in the Women's Residence Hall. (Photo by Brown, Beaver, Pa.; Beaver Area Historical Museum)

1923 tuition receipt of Grace M. Muse '27. Miss Muse was one of the students who moved with the College from Beaver to Jenkintown, Pa. in 1925. (Arcadia University Archives)

Dravo baseball field. (Photo
by Brown, Beaver, Pa.; Beaver
Area Historical Museum)

The gymnasium in
College Hall. (Beaver Area
Historical Museum)

1902 baseball team on the steps of College Hall. (Beaver Area Historical Museum)

1909 women's basketball team.
(Arcadia University Archives)

1903 men's basketball team.
(Beaver Area Historical Museum)

Miss Elizabeth Reed '03, Editor
(third seated person from the
left) and the Editorial Board of
The Beaver in 1903. (Beaver
Area Historical Museum)

The Trustees, Faculty and Senior
Class of Beaver College

request the honor of your presence
at the events of

Commencement Week

from Wednesday, the third of June
to Monday, the eighth of June

nineteen hundred twenty-five
Beaver, Pennsylvania

FROM FEMALE SEMINARY TO COMPREHENSIVE UNIVERSITY

PART III: A NEW BEGINNING IN THE EAST 1925–1953

Ruth L. Higgins and Mary S. Sturgeon

The whole is more than the sum of its parts. Beaver College, from 1927 until 1962, operated two campuses, one in Jenkintown and the other in Glenside, Pennsylvania. Students lived at both sites and were bused between campuses for classes and social events.

The "Beaver Bus" transported students between the Jenkintown and Glenside campuses. (Arcadia University Archives)

A NEW BEGINNING
IN THE EAST 1925–1953

To Jenkintown came only a token of the institution founded in 1853—a handful of students,

President Harris; Miss Alice Reed, Home Economics; Miss Catherine Buhrmester, Science;

and Dr. C. Mace Thomas, Psychology, Philosophy and Education; the library of 10,000 volumes,

equipment for chemistry, biology, and physics laboratories, and a few articles of furnishings.

President Harris remained to help organize the combined curricula, to pilot through to state approval the teaching certification of degree graduates, and to see negotiations with the Presbyterian Church to a point where its adoption of the college seemed assured. Then he resigned, having contributed faithfully to the persistence of the institution founded so long before, so long threatened with foundering for lack of support in spite of its record of distinguished service to the education of women.

Beechwood, a junior college and preparatory school, had been opened in 1912 by Dr. Matthew Reaser, an educator whose experience included that of President of Lindenwood and of Wilson College. Its purpose was two-fold: to offer opportunities for young women to pursue their cultural studies, and to prepare them at the same time for training in such practical work as they might elect. The curricula included certificate courses in fine arts, music, expression, normal gymnastic education, home economics, domestic arts, and secretaryship . . . .

Dr. C. Mace Thomas, who came to Beaver in 1910, remained until his death in 1936 the living link between the two eras in the history of Beaver College . . . . In the last years of the institution in Beaver, he served not only as Professor of Psychology, Philosophy, and Education, Dean of Faculty, and Acting President (1919–1921) but also as field representative, and ably carried on the determination of the College not to relax its academic standards in spite of the competition for students. . . .

In 1928, Beaver called a new president whose vigor and ambition were to make the college more widely known and to greatly influence its fortunes for a long time, the Reverend Walter Burton Greenway, prominent Presbyterian clergyman . . . . Under Dr. Greenway, every area of the college was improved and enlarged. A new dormitory had been opened in 1926. But it was apparent soon that the expansion of the college to care adequately for the fuller life of even the limited enrollment of six hundred required a new campus of more than the approximately

Dr. C. Mace Thomas, Professor of Psychology, Philosophy, and Education (1910–1936); Acting President (1919–1921); and Dean of the Faculty (1921–1925). (Arcadia University Archives)

Beechwood Hall was the main building of the Beechwood School in Jenkintown. After the merger of Beechwood School and Beaver College, the building's name was changed to Beaver Hall. It was used as a residence hall and also housed faculty and administrative offices. The dining hall was located in one wing. Before being purchased by the Beechwood School, the building was a resort hotel. (Arcadia University Archives)

The Jenkintown campus circa 1930. (Arcadia University Archives)

Grey Towers Castle, the main building on the Glenside campus, showing the south side of the building and the conservatory that once stood on the patio. The conservatory was torn down in the 1950s because it was deemed unsafe without major repairs that were too expensive to undertake. (Arcadia University Archives)

The Glenside campus circa 1930. The structures below Grey Towers Castle are greenhouses that no longer exist. (Arcadia University Archives)

eleven acres and the buildings in Jenkintown. The first step to meet this need was the purchase by the trustees of the estate in Glenside known as Grey Towers which with its stone buildings, streams, and rolling lawns provided a campus of rare beauty. By the fall of 1929 the buildings of the original estate had been converted to care for sixty-five resident students and provide laboratories for chemistry, biology, and physics . . . .

Less happy for the future of the college was the fiscal situation confronting Dr. Raymon M. Kistler when, in the summer of 1940, he was called to be president, Dr. Greenway having resigned in 1939 and Mr. James E. Mooney having remained in the interim as acting president. Under the new president, plans for raising capital funds to save and develop the institution, which had long suffered under deficit financing and the heavy ground rent, were initiated but had to be postponed because of the advent of war. Under the jurisdiction of the court the College passed through a period of reorganization, during which Dr. Kistler served as part-time president and the administration was under-staffed in other respects as well. But the faculty almost to the last member stood by and the College emerged solvent and in perhaps the soundest financial position of its long history [to that point] . . . .

Under by-laws adopted by the faculty in 1943 and amended by it since, much of the academic work of the College needed for full faculty action is carried on by joint committees functioning with mutual respect. Under Dr. Kistler's administration the College achieved a stable, respected position almost free of the tremendous debt which threatened to bury it . . . .

Throughout the tenuous years of the war and reorganization, Dr. Morgan Thomas, president of the Board, proved himself even more firmly than ever the friend of Beaver, supporting the administration both morally and financially to limits of incalculable worth. His latest large benefaction was the assumption of the mortgage on Grey Towers with Mrs. Clifford Heinz, secretary of the Board and long herself a generous benefactor of the college . . . .

Curricular Changes

Before 1934, the A.B. and B.S. were given for the Liberal Arts Curriculum, the B.S. in Education for programs in General Education, Elementary Education, Kindergarten-Primary Education, Commercial Education and Secretaryship, Home Economics Education, and Health Education; and the Mus.B. and B.F.A. for appropriate curricula. In 1934–1935 the degrees were reduced and simplified to A.B., B.S., Mus.B., and B.F.A . . . .

In 1934–1935 special attention to needed curricular changes especially in the professional program was given by the new academic dean [Dr. Ruth Higgins] and faculty committees. The Liberal Arts requirements were strengthened, new courses were added, and inadequate and out-of-date courses were eliminated in the successful

Dr. Raymon Kistler, President
(1940–1960). (Photo by
Bachrach, Philadelphia, Pa.;
Arcadia University Archives)

REMINISCENCES OF BEAVER COLLEGE [12]

Raymon Kistler

I knew full well [upon assuming the presidency in 1940] that our major problem was financial, but I hesitated to engage in any active solicitation until I felt better acquainted with the [College's] total program. In about a year, we had a [fundraising] program lined up with the "kick off" dinner in the dining room of Grey Towers. The next week came Pearl Harbor and our entry into the war. Naturally, that ended that campaign . . . . As the enrollment of men sharply declined in men's colleges, women's colleges also slipped, but Beaver opened that fall with about 450 enrolled, which at that time was considered a respectable total.

In October, I made my usual call on one of the banks, which had been financing Beaver in recent years. We had just paid in full all the short term notes we had given to this bank, where the President of our Board of Trustees was a director, and to the other much larger Bank, where another of our Board members was the President. The larger bank had always allowed the smaller one to set the total of the obligations, which was the reason for making that my first stop. I will never forget that hour. After reminding him that our notes had been paid in full, I guess I somewhat casually asked him if we could count on the same total of credit for the new semester. He had always been very friendly and he was still friendly, but in essence, this is what he said, "College operation today is a precarious business. Many institutions are being taken over, in whole or in part, by the Government, and we have been warned by Washington that short-term loans to colleges in anticipation of future receipts cannot be considered sound." I asked, "Does that mean that our line of credit will be reduced?" Answer, "I am not sure that we will be able to make you any loans. In face of warnings received from above, if for any reason you were unable to repay the loans, the directors who voted for them would be held individually responsible and would have to make up any deficit."

At that moment, I was in no condition to go on to the other bank as I had intended. I could easily see the end of Beaver. I meekly explained to the banker that we have 450 girls who had paid their tuition for the semester and that more than half of them had paid for room and board. His reply, apparently ending the conference was, "Doctor, I have plenty of problems of my own, but that one is yours!" But I do know that they had a meeting of their board at the College later and discussed our situation, but with no helpful results.

In the meantime I went back to the College, gathered all the administrative officers available and shared the gloom with them. Nobody had $50,000 available, but you can be sure we agreed to give the situation our best. I will not bother you with

[12] These passages are excerpted from an unpublished manuscript entitled "Reminiscences of Beaver College" written by Dr. Raymon Kistler soon after his retirement in 1960.

my feelings in the days that followed, but you can possibly guess when I was carrying around in my pocket an announcement I was prepared to make any day to a specially called meeting of the student body, explaining that we had spent all their money, had no cash to buy food for the dining-room, and they might as well go home.

But some bright spots appeared. When I reported the situation at the Faculty meeting, they unanimously agreed that we were obligated to complete the semester, at least. All agreed to serve at half salary. The larger bank came to the rescue with a loan of enough money to cover the food bills, realizing that it might all go down the drain. One of the women members of the faculty came to the office and told me that she had been blessed in receiving thousands of dollars, that Beaver College was her life, that if the college closed her money would mean nothing to her, and that she wanted me to accept all her funds to help us through our current difficulties. I certainly appreciated her sacrificial spirit, but under the circumstances I could not accept. I went downtown and outlined our situation to the Board of Christian Education. It was rather disillusioning to have them tell me how sorry they were, but that when the College closed, they would have a position for me with the Board!

Although the students surely knew that something was wrong, many of them assured us that they were going to enroll for the next semester. We could not take their payments at that time, because some of our creditors had entered judgments against us and their money would have to be applied on those bills . . . .

One of the critical moments of the period occurred when the Registrar [Miss Roberta Paulhamus] came in to my office and asked if I would have any objection to her discussing our problem with one of her professors at Temple University. She had been attending their Law School at night . . . . She was currently taking a course in bankruptcy and felt that there was a chance that taking advantage of the legal provision for voluntary bankruptcy might pull us through. I was not only glad to give the requested permission, but suggested that if her professor felt it would be feasible, to ask him if he would be willing to represent us in instituting such a proceeding. When she reported the result of that interview, she was all enthused. He felt we had a good chance, and if the Board of Trustees approved of the procedure, would be glad to take our case.

The Board did approve; he became our attorney and filed the necessary application in the United States Court before Judge Welsh. We found the Judge very understanding, and quite familiar with the problems of higher education as he was a member of the Board of Trustees of Temple University, and I believe at that time, its Vice President. He appointed a Master who interviewed me for a couple of hours and recommended the granting of the petition. There were more meetings and Court appearances, then the petition was approved, and Beaver became responsible to the Court. A Mr. Kenworthy and I were appointed Trustees in Reorganization, reporting to Judge Welsh. He issued an order that the College should continue the second semester, but that all money paid in by the students must be used only for their board and education. That meant that

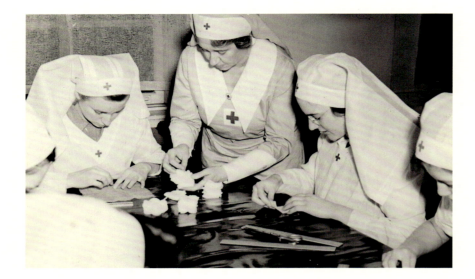

Beaver College students
became members of
the Wyncote Unit of the
Southeastern Pennsylvania
Chapter of the American Red
Cross during World War II.
(Arcadia University Archives)

all obligations and bills, previously contracted, were frozen and we were making a fresh start. The Faculty again was paid in full. Most of our suppliers continued to serve us, but usually on a cash basis. We opened a new account at the bank under the title "Estate of Beaver College, debtor for Bankruptcy cause" and every check we issued carried the legend in large letters, "ESTATE OF BEAVER COLLEGE" and was only valid when signed by me and Mr. Kenworthy. When he was at the Shore on vacation, we had to take the checks down to him. We reported regularly to the Judge, but as Mr. Kenworthy was a friend of Judge Welsh and had lunch with him regularly, he carried that responsibility.

Except for the name on the checks, there was no outward sign of our difficulty. Our Board of Trustees had no responsibilities, but continued to meet regularly to consider possible ways of terminating the receivership, which meant the satisfying of all creditors. Neither the Judge or Mr. Kenworthy interfered in the routine operation of the College, which left it pretty much up to me, and I worked closely with our important Trustees.

Another critical moment in the period came when we were having a meeting of the Board at the Union League. The largest item of our indebtedness was the mortgage of $265,000. We felt sure that the holder of the mortgage would accept a reduced payment, under the circumstances. During the meeting, Dr. Morgan Thomas and Mrs. Vira Heinz went to a corner for a private conversation and returned with the happy suggestion that they would be willing to take over the entire Grey Towers mortgage.

They explained that because of tax complications, they would not turn the mortgage over to the College as a whole at present, but would each hold half of it at a low rate of interest, would write into their wills a provision that at their death the mortgage would go to the College, and would possibly make annual payments on it. You can be sure that this offer was accepted with enthusiasm by the Board and I can now tell you that they have each paid off their share, so that the original Towers property was free of encumbrance . . . .

So Beaver was able to continue, enrollment increased, few vacancies occurred in the Faculty, and I was given free hand to fill those, which I did in conference with the department heads.

Our creditors organized a committee and selected lawyers to confer with our lawyers. It seemed to us to take a lot of time, but at last an agreement was reached. Judge Welsh called a meeting of all concerned in his courtroom. It was announced that the creditors group would be willing to settle outstanding obligations for 25 cents on the dollar, that the College would be able to clear up its indebtedness on that basis. Judge Welsh expressed his happiness at the successful culmination of the action, thanked all who had participated, discharged the Trustees in Reorganization, who had been serving under the direction of the court and declared the bankruptcy terminated. He ordered the regular Trustees of the College to resume their usual responsibilities. Beaver was on its own and on its way!

efforts to reorganize curricula to meet acceptable standards of state departments, graduate schools, and other accrediting agencies . . . .

Special pre-professional fields other than preparation for teaching were evolved . . . . For example, a separate option for students in dietetics was created for Home Economics. In later years a general option was added for students specializing in foods or clothing for home or commercial purposes. The former secretaryship program was replaced by one in Business Administration which included suitable advanced courses . . . .

In the curricula of Liberal Arts, some changes were made in 1934–1935 in the general and departmental requirements and from time to time additional major fields were made available. Instead of a separate Christian Education program, Bible and Religious Education became in 1934–1935 a major field in Liberal Arts. Music and Fine Arts were also added to the list of majors for students not interested in the intensive applied work required by the special degrees. Within a few years major fields of Psychology and Social Welfare were added. Later on interdepartmental majors in Languages and Literatures and in American Civilization were made available.

In 1937 the faculty committee on curricula revised the general education requirements of the Liberal Arts program and placed them on a group selection basis. The minor field as a requirement for the degree was eliminated in 1942 and the major fields of concentration developed to include a major of approximately 24 to 30 credits plus selected subjects to total approximately 48 credits. The last important revision of the curriculum in Liberal Arts was made to strengthen the science and history requirements for the degree, in line with the request of the AAUW [American Association of University Women] and the general education trends among reputable colleges . . . .

Accrediting

Academically, the most important goal was membership in the Middle States Association of Colleges and Secondary Schools. Dr. William E. Weld, President of Wells College, made the first inspection in 1937 and Dr. Greenway and the Dean of the College then appeared before the Commission on Higher Education at Princeton. Although the financial condition of the College prevented acceptance for membership, the report indicated approval of the academic program.

The inspection in 1939 by Dr. Eugene Bradford, Director of Admissions at Cornell University, was helpful academically but was somewhat perfunctory inasmuch as Beaver College had only an acting president at that time. Dr. Weld made another inspection in 1941, but in the war period the financial situation again blocked approval. In 1945, when the academic dean was attending the inauguration of the President of Lafayette College, Dr. Weld, a true friend of Beaver, asked permission to

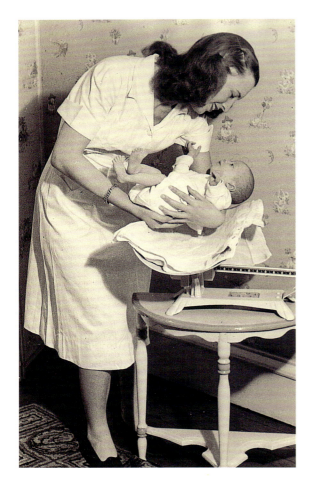

A Home Economics student caring for a baby. As part of her senior laboratory requirements, each Home Economics student was required to take total care of an infant for one week. The infant was "on loan" from a local orphanage and lived in a nursery in Highland Hall on the Jenkintown campus. (Arcadia University Archives)

Freshmen arriving on the Jenkintown campus circa 1932. (Arcadia University Archives)

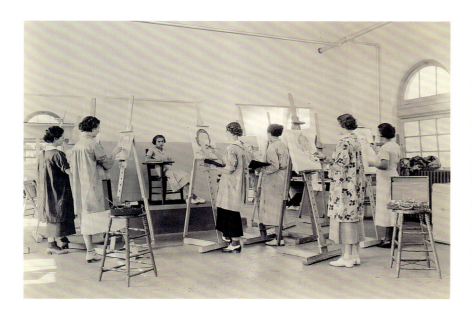

re-inspect the college before his retirement from the Commission. The material was hastily brought up-to-date for his inspection a short time later. The financial condition of the College having been greatly improved under President Kistler, the long awaited goal of approval was achieved in the spring of 1946 . . . .

Beaver College became a member of the Association of American Colleges in 1940, the American Council on Education in 1947, and in October, 1950, the College Entrance Examination Board. The alumnae were particularly concerned with approval by the American Association of University Women. Application had been made by the Dean of the College in 1934, but because Beaver for a time lacked approval by the appropriate academic agencies and because the voluntary Committee on Standards of the Association had a back-log of requests for inspection, a visit from the AAUW representatives was not possible until March, 1952. Notice of the approval came in May of that year . . . .

Enrollment

In 1925–1926 there were 325 enrolled for the College. At the same time there were also 40 students in the preparatory work, but this program was given up within a few years and the enrollment for the College steadily increased. The student body became more national, there being many states and a number of foreign countries represented. The peak [pre-war] enrollment was reached in 1937–1938 with 701 students . . . . The lowest point in enrollment came in the war years, particularly in 1943–1944 when only 447 students were registered.

Three years later Beaver College had its largest freshman class to [that] date. A summer session was held first in 1932 aimed to meet the needs of the regular students, and to enable teachers . . . to continue work toward a degree or to meet the latest certification requirements. In 1948 Dr. John Wallace organized a European field trip program in comparative economics . . . .[13]

Buildings

In . . . [1935], Brookside Hall on the Grey Towers campus, (formerly the engineer's building) [later named Spruance Hall] was equipped for Fine Arts. Earlier this department had been located in Beaver Hall [on the Jenkintown campus] . . . . Gradually the Fine Arts department expanded into two of the adjoining buildings, Commercial Design and Fashion Illustration in one and Interior Design and Architecture in the other. The Little Theater was housed in one of these buildings enabling classes to work together for the programs in Fine Arts and Theatre.

Because of an increase in student enrollment . . . additional dormitory space was provided for 1936–1937. Highland Hall, formerly used for faculty, West Lodge (a rented house on the opposite corner), Greenwood Lodge,

---

[13] This trip was the beginning of what would become the Center for Education Abroad, see pp. 164–171.

Social Regulations

1. A student who wishes to leave the College to be absent for one meal or more obtains permission from her Social Directress before leaving and reports upon her return.

2. Permission for callers, excursions, or weekends away is not given unless the student presents a request or approval from parent or guardian.

3. Students do not leave the campus after dinner without a chaperone, except as hereafter provided, nor do they visit physicians' or dentists' offices unchaperoned. This includes attendance upon entertainments into city at night.

4. All students may go walking in groups of two or more, to Jenkintown, from 8 A. M. to 6 P. M. on weekends. Signing out and in is required each time at your Social Office.

5. Students may go automobiling under chaperonage of Faculty, with permission of the Social Directress.

6. If a student finds it impossible to be on the campus by 6 P. M., she shall telephone her Social Directress, and on her arrival report to her Social Directress.

7. Students may not go unchaperoned without permission to "friends" unless such friends are registered on the books of her Social Directress and approved.

8. Parties of less than four must not take long walks unchaperoned. Registration must be made with their Social Office.

9. Students must not go off the campus on Sunday afternoon unless with special permission. Special permission will be granted for walking on Sunday afternoon. The Sabbath must be observed in keeping with its sacred character.

10. All students are required to return to the College from weekends and elsewhere on Sunday by 7.25 P. M.

11. Ice cream and candy may be delivered at 10 P. M.

12. No man shall be taken to the dormitory floors by students—the only exception being a father. Social Office must be notified of parents visits.

13. Students visiting outside dormitories must sign before leaving and on returning after 6 P. M.

14. No unnecessary interference with study hours shall be permitted. Social privileges and entertainments shall be arranged as far as possible for Friday after classes and Saturday.

15. SMOKING IS ABSOLUTELY PROHIBITED. Anyone violating this rule will be dealt with severely.

16. *Callers.* Student may receive callers on Friday and Saturday evenings from 8–10.30 and Sunday for dinner, and from 2–4.30 P. M., if they have filed a written permission from parents or guardian, with the Social Directress.

(a) All guests having meals must be signed for in the Social Office by their hostesses before entering the dining room.

(b) When expecting a caller a guest card must be filed—name of caller placed on it—and filed with the Social Office. This must be done before the caller is received.

(c) All callers must be presented to your Social Directress.

(d) Callers *leave the building* at the ringing of the bell at 10 P. M. Failure on the part of the caller to observe this rule will result in withdrawal of the calling privilege from the student hostess.

Source
Beaver College Handbook, 1929–'30. Beaver College Self-Government Association

The Chatterbox, the student snack bar, was located in Beaver Hall on the Jenkintown campus. "Chat," the current name for the student snack bar, is a shortened version of the original. (Arcadia University Archives)

behind Huntington Hall, originally used for faculty, and Florence Lodge (formerly and now the President's house) were all used for student housing. The Lodge, the Gate House on the Grey Towers campus, was named Glen Lodge in 1936 [and later, Blake Hall]. In succeeding years it was sometimes used as a French House.

For 1937–1938 the two wings of Montgomery Hall were available and the dormitory capacity accommodations of that building were increased from 66 to 134. This addition enabled the College to give up some of the small lodges. Furthermore, the Home Economics House, which in 1938 had been in a rented house on Greenwood Avenue, was established at Highland Hall . . . . Beaver Hall, once a summer hotel for the carriage trade, underwent many changes through the years. The Infirmary was once in what became the dining room. Space for the business offices was increased by enclosing the inner porch. The post office and the bookstore, located in the present space of the Admissions Office (for a time a classroom) were moved to the ground floor near the Chatterbox. With the Athletic Association headquarters, smoking lounge, and maintenance office nearby, this area developed into a popular activity and service center.

Grey Towers campus was acquired in 1929. The main building with its stone towers and battlements, its gargoyles and grotesques, is a replica of an old world castle [Alnwick Castle, the medieval seat of the Duke of Northumberland, in England]. Inside the three-storied baronial hall, art and craftsmanship in wood and stone and in tapestry and other decorations remain to reflect the lavish taste of its original owner. The Castle is used as a social center and for dormitory purposes.[14] The former stables of the Harrison family [later called Murphy Hall] included well-equipped laboratories in chemistry, physics, and biology, as well as a large auditorium and gymnasium. The spacious grounds provided an attractive center for May Day pageants and outdoor Commencement services.

Student Activities

. . . Student activities outside the classroom have been notable for their adjustment to the changing tastes and needs of the passing generations of [undergraduates]. Student self-government at Beaver has provided through the years a convincing expression of democracy in action. Indeed, it has been and is one of the most cheering realities in the life of the College. Through its inclusive and therefore intricate organization, kept responsive to the will of succeeding college generations of students, it has demonstrated the ability of those chosen by their fellow students to lead them and the collective wisdom of the students themselves . . . . The academic honor system developed and administered by honor council was enviable and a source of pride to all friends of Beaver . . . .

| [14] See the essay "Grey Towers Castle" on pp. 144–153 for more details.

Pin awarded to students who served on the Forum Committee. (Photo by Jerome Lukowicz, Philadelphia, Pa.; Arcadia University Archives)

During the early thirties departmental clubs multiplied greatly. Extra-curricular activities, needing de-emphasis and placed under control of a student-faculty committee in 1940, and in 1941 largely coordinated by a Forum of Arts and Sciences, continued to develop constructively to combine practice with the theory of the classroom. Since 1925 the students of journalism and creative writing have had practical experience in preparing for publication the *Periscope* (1925–1926), the *Campus Crier* (1926–1929), the *Beaver College News*, (1929–1930), and the *Beaver News* (begun in 1935 and continuing to 1953) [student newspapers]; . . . the *Beaver Review* [a literary magazine] organized . . . in the thirties; . . . the *Beaver Log* (formerly the *Beechbark*) [yearbooks]; and the *Student Handbook* . . . . The *Beaver Review* brought to the college and the community such famous persons as William Butler Yeats, Edna St. Vincent Millay, Robert Frost, Thorton Wilder, Stephen Leacock, Hugh Walpole, Cornelia Otis Skinner, Pearl Buck, Robert P. Tristam Coffin, and Carl Sandburg . . . .

One college-wide honor society, Lambda Delta Alpha, and five departmental honor societies functioned at Beaver. Lambda Delta Alpha, organized in 1932 . . . was the senior honor society and membership in it was the highest academic honor awarded at Beaver. In 1941 Beaver acquired a chapter of Psi Chi, honor society in psychology, and through the efforts of the staff of the student publications, a chapter of Pi Delta Epsilon,

national fraternity in journalism, was established in 1938. Kappa Delta Pi, national education society, was first represented at Beaver in 1948, and a chapter of Alpha Kappa Alpha, honor society in philosophy, was formed in 1938. Pentathlon recognized honors in athletics and Alpha Psi Omega in dramatics . . . .

Music provided extracurricular interest in participation for a large part of the student body of Beaver . . . . In 1913 a glee club was organized at Beaver and there is a record of a music club at Beechwood School in 1918. A merged Glee Club was formed in 1925, and in 1935 W. Lawrence Curry took over the directorship. The club presented joint concerts with the orchestra of Harvard University and with the glee clubs of Haverford, Franklin and Marshall, Lehigh, Lafayette, Princeton, and others and sang in many churches of the Philadelphia area, over radio and on television, at the Lehigh Music Festival, and in its own annual concerts, for several years heard in Town Hall, Philadelphia. At various times a college choir provided music for the regular services on campus, for years on Sunday night, and for the Christmas and Easter vespers, besides appearing in churches of the area.

. . . Beclex (Beaver College Expression Club) of 1926, [and the later] Theater Playshop saw many successful productions of conventional plays as well as considerable success in the experimental theatre, notably in the world premiere of Gertrude Stein's *Dr. Faustus*

Grey Towers on the
Glenside campus.
(Arcadia University Archives)

Freshmen proclaim their status
in the Chatterbox on the
Jenkintown campus circa 1938.
(Arcadia University Archives)

Beaver College pennant circa
1946. (Photo by Jerome
Lukowicz, Philadelphia, Pa.;
Arcadia University Archives)

A vinyl record of the junior class during the 1948 Song Contest. Students often produced such permanent recordings of the popular annual event. (Photo by Jerome Lukowicz, Philadelphia, Pa.; Arcadia University Archives)

Lights the Lights in 1951. Beclex also sponsored the first inter-class play contest, and through Beclex and Theatre Playshop, opportunities have been found for interested students in radio and television . . . .

All students of Beaver were members of the Athletic Association, which undertook to develop interest in sports and create a spirit of good sportsmanship, and which supervised organized athletic activities. The Association had as its forerunners the athletic clubs of the older Beaver and especially of Beechwood. These groups sponsored varsity teams in various sports and had as their primary aims the promotion of sports and health. By 1928 the athletics group was sponsoring such other activities as musicals ("Marryin' Marian," 1928), dances, and teas.

For many years, under the guidance of members of the Health and Physical Education Department, major and non-major students have excelled in intercollegiate competition, competing in [field] hockey, basketball, softball, golf, and riflery with such rivals as Bryn Mawr, Ursinus, Swarthmore, Drexel, New York University, University of Pennsylvania, Temple University, and William and Mary. In hockey, golf, and riflery Beaver has produced star performers and teams of national prominence.

The reorganization of Beaver upon the move to Jenkintown was so radical that the institution with respect to customs and traditions was new rather than old, although some of the Beechwood traditions inevitably remained when Beaver College established itself on the Beechwood campus. With the expansion of 1928 came a desire of the students to broaden their college life, which made them particularly aware of the lack of customs and traditions peculiar to Beaver. The class of 1933 is credited with originating the custom of wearing the traditional green beanies or caps for freshman orientation.

The most cherished of all Beaver traditions or customs and the most popularly attended by the friends of the College and maintained by students old and new was the annual song contest held each year on the night before Thanksgiving vacation. Song Contest originated in 1932 to provide Beaver with songs to be used at "pep" meetings and athletic contests. During the middle years of its history the event threatened to supercede academic matters in emphasis, for practice was without limit. Eventually, the time allowed each class for rehearsal was limited, without damage to the quality of the performances. Items presented in competition by the four classes were a "pep" song, an Alma Mater, and a class song with original words and music.

In the Murphy Hall Gymnasium the classes participated in the order of their minority to the refrain of tremendous applause, and excitement and enthusiasm were rampant. While judges, outstanding musicians, were out making their decision, the seniors sang an original class hymn (first introduced in 1928) and then entertained the audience, traditionally in excess of seating capacity, with old songs. Then the freshman class amid

stamping of feet and the rhythmic shout of "tip," tossed their green beanies on a pile and become fraternally [sic] a permanent part of Beaver. The silver cup, presented by Dr. Morgan Thomas in 1937, was awarded to the class giving the best performance. The Glee Club cup was awarded for the best song, the E. Reed Shutt cup for the most original and clever song, and honorable mention went to the class that presented the second best performance. After mutual congratulations, the classes returned to the Jenkintown campus for a huge bonfire and "Coke" feast with the winning class drinking toasts from the loving cup and good fellowship abounding generally. The class of 1949 had the honor of being the only one to win song contest all four years of its participation.

Among the traditional events was Founders' Day. Although Beaver College was founded on December 28, this day was traditionally observed as an academic event in September in connection with the formal opening of the College . . . . Degrees were granted at this time as well as at the June commencement service. Other traditional events were Honors Day, a convocation instituted in 1936 as Scholarship Day at which academic honors of the students were acclaimed; the President's reception; Fun Week, the culmination of freshman hazing; the freshman dance, the sophomore hop, the junior promenade, the senior ball, and other senior week festivities; the senior-junior ring breakfast; senior-faculty dinner; and the colorful and elaborate festival of May Day.

Since its founding, Beaver College has been church-related, except for . . . [The period between its disaffiliation from the Methodist Church in 1925], and 1928, when it was approved for inclusion in its list of recognized colleges by the State Synod and the Board of Christian Education of the Presbyterian Church, U.S.A. It was the policy of the College to engage faculty members who belonged to some evangelical Christian church and all students were required to take a Bible course each year and to attend Chapel services regularly . . . .

The students represented many different denominations and they were encouraged to attend churches or synagogues of their choice. All students attended brief chapel vespers two evenings a week and a longer service, addressed often by a visiting clergyman, on Monday nights. The Y.W.C.A. continued upon the original charter granted in 1906. The Student Volunteer Group, a part of a nationwide organization, was formed on campus in 1948 by students interested in church service and missionary work. Branches of the League of Evangelical Students and the League of Christian Students were active in 1935 and 1936. The Canterbury Club was made up of student members of the Episcopal church. Catholic students met together in the Newman Club, founded in 1938, and Jewish students in a similar organization, Hillel, founded in 1951.

Through faculty and student participation as well as through curriculum changes Beaver College took its part

Coach Linford D. Schober with Beaver College's 1948 National Women's Intercollegiate Championship rifle team. (Photo by Harry J. Utzy, Jenkintown, Pa.; Arcadia University Archives)

BEAVER COLLEGE'S ANNIE OAKLEYS

The Beaver College rifle team was formed as a club during the 1935–36 academic year. It became an intercollegiate team and had its first official match on January 7, 1937, against a highly experienced team from the Frankford Arsenal, Philadelphia. Beaver lost, but by only two points, a very auspicious beginning to a brilliant era. The coach was Linford D. Schober, an outstanding marksman who had won numerous medals in national, state and local competition. The rifle range was located first in Murphy Hall gymnasium on the Glenside campus and, in later years, in the basement of Huntington Hall on the Jenkintown campus.

By 1938, Mr. Schober felt that some of his riflewomen were ready for national competition and entered Eleanor Lum '40, Anne Jendryk '38, and Virginia Junkin '38, in the Women's United States Amateur Championship match. Eleanor Lum won the championship with a score of 598 out of a possible 600. The most remarkable aspect of this triumph was that she had no experience in riflery when she came to Beaver as a freshman. Virginia Junkin won sixth place while Anne Jendryk won the Pennsylvania State championship.

By 1939, the team regularly competed in the National Women's Intercollegiate Championships. In matches from 1939 through 1951, Beaver College's team always finished in among the top three teams. In 1948, still coached by Mr. Schober, the team won its first National Championship. The members of the championship team were: Rosemarie Bahn '48, Elizabeth Flanagan '50, Barbara Klein '50, Nancy Mitchell '50, and Margaret Mitchell '50. Margaret Mitchell also won the overall college championship. The team was so good that the U. S. Marine Corps squad challenged the Beaver women to a match. Much to the Marines' chagrin, they lost by a score of 979 to 973.

In 1950 and 1951 the team repeated its stellar performance winning the National Women's Intercollegiate Championship in both years. Top scorers Nancy Mitchell '50 and Marilyn Johnson '52, both of whom obtained a score of 496 out of a possible 500, led the 1950 team to victory. The top scorer in the 1951 Nationals was Virginia Fulmer '51, with 498 points out of a possible 500. The team shot 2,474 out of a possible 2,500 points. Of the five members of the 1951 championship team only one, Virginia Fulmer, had any experience in riflery before coming to Beaver College.

Coach Schober retired in the spring of 1953. The sport was temporarily discontinued and never revived. *Samuel M. Cameron*

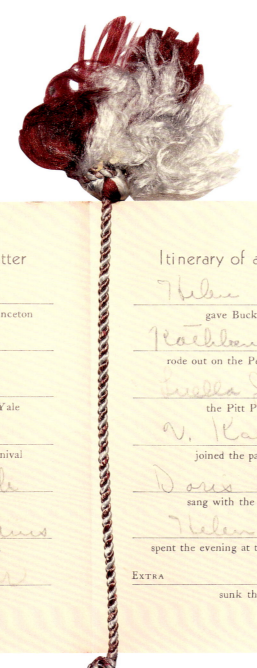

Itinerary of a Prom Trotter

Helen
_____
went to do the "Tiger Rag" at Princeton

_____
hopped on at Rutgers

Helen
_____
greeted us with a hey—ho! from Yale

Trude
_____
cut a figure at the Dartmouth Carnival

Molly Smith
_____
had a lampoon at Harvard

Kathleen Kauus
_____
went yodeling on Lake Cayuga

Extra _Aida Bonner_
_____
certainly got Navy's goat

INTERMISSION

Itinerary of a Prom Trotter

Helen
_____
gave Bucknell a break

Kathleen
_____
rode out on the Penn State lion to see

Luella Judson
_____
the Pitt Panther with

V. Kachel
_____
joined the party at Lehigh

Doris Stone
_____
sang with the Lafayette Lyre

Helen
_____
spent the evening at the Penn Punch Bowl

Extra
_____
sunk the Army

Dance card for the Senior
Ball of the Class of 1930.
(Photo by Jerome Lukowicz,
Philadelphia, Pa.; Arcadia
University Archives)

84

Jacqueline Stroher '53, Centennial Queen (on left), President Raymon Kistler and Beverly Gifford '53, President of the Student Government Association (on right) cut the centennial cake. (Arcadia University Archives)

in the war effort of the years 1941–1945. Out of a faculty-student committee, headed by President Kistler, were formed three departments to organize activity: (1) the Department of Better Understanding, to help explain the reasons behind the war-aims and the conditions necessary for true peace; (2) the Department of Personal Service; and (3) the Department of Financial Assistance. Realizing the need for students to be prepared for the world situation, the faculty made various curriculum changes, among these new courses in history and government and accelerated courses in languages. In 1942 the college program was accelerated by the elimination of final examinations and most vacations to release students and faculty as early as May 16 for a long summer of war work. Further, in the fall of 1943, a two-year "Victory Course" was offered, giving diplomas for the following programs: nursery school teaching, laboratory technique, recreational leadership, physical therapy, drafting, and secretarial sciences.

Centennial Year

The year 1953 was observed as the Centennial Year of Beaver College. During this time a special fund raising campaign to provide for the construction of additional buildings on the Grey Towers campus was the special concern of all interested in the future of the College and [it] received generous contributions from many of them . . . . Numerous events emphasized the Centennial theme. In January, a Centennial Dinner was given in Town Hall on the 8th and the President's Reception at Grey Towers on the 16th. The Junior Promenade events on February 13 and 14 made use of the Centennial motif. In March, Shakespeare's *The Winter's Tale*, produced by the Theatre Playshop, The Beaver Night Program, presented by the Glee Club in conjunction with Lafayette, and an exhibition by the Fine Arts Department provided a highly successful Fine Arts Festival.

The students arranged a special Parent's Day for April 11 and the radio program Town Meeting of the Air was broadcast from Beaver on April 7. The May Day celebration took the form of an historical pageant, and on the 7th the Special Academic Convocation, with guests from neighboring colleges and universities was held with Dr. Milton Eisenhower, president of the Pennsylvania State College, delivering the main address.

The alumnae celebrated the Centennial by holding a very special reunion on June 6 and 7. Participating in commencement exercises on June 7 was an honor guard of alumnae representing all classes from 1894 to 1953. At the Baccalaureate exercises Dr. Kistler delivered the sermon, and Mr. Charles E. Wilson, one-time director of defense mobilization and former president of General Electric Company, was the speaker at commencement exercises.

THE POT AT THE END OF THE RAINBOW

AN ESSAY

Samuel M. Cameron

William Curran, M.D.
(Image courtesy of the
C. Elizabeth Boyd '33
Archives, Wilson College)

In 1925, Beaver College moved east from Beaver to Jenkintown, Pa. In 1928, the College began its affiliation with the Presbyterian Church, USA. What motivated the institution to make these changes? A critical factor was a large estate left by William Curran, M. D. It appears that the College was in search of a pot of gold at the end of a rainbow in the vicinity of Philadelphia.

Dr. William Curran, a wealthy Philadelphia physician, was also a devout Presbyterian. He received his medical degree in 1848 from the University of Pennsylvania and became a successful physician, but always felt guilty that he had not followed the calling of his youth to become a missionary. In his will, he created a fund, "the annual income of which shall be used to promote the higher education of females, in an institution adapted to that purpose, which shall be located in the City of Philadelphia or adjacent to it." He directed that the college should instruct these women in literature and, in particular, the Bible and Greek and Latin. The scholarships were to go to: daughters of foreign missionaries, daughters of ministers of the gospel, daughters of the learned professions, and finally, women who "give evidence of talents which may adorn society and bless the world." Later in the document he reiterated, "it is my will to devote all of my means, after the decease of my dear wife, to the gratuitous education of young women in my beloved Philadelphia . . . . If no such female college exists, I have confidence that one will soon arise to meet the necessity." The income of the estate was to be used to support such goals when the value of his investments reached $500,000 or produced an annual income of $30,000. He further requested the Presbyterian Church's "Synod of Philadelphia to have an oversight of the progress of this endowment."

Dr. Curran died in 1880 and his will was probated in 1883. The Synod established a committee, consisting of twelve ruling Elders, to monitor the progress of the Curran Fund. The Fidelity-Philadelphia Trust Company, as Trustee of the Curran Estate, followed Dr. Curran's instructions in his will and over the years the value of the estate increased until, in the late 1920s, it approached the point where the estate was free of all encumbrances and earning an annual income of $30,000. As the Fund approached this point it triggered a series of court battles in which Beaver College was a participant.

The College had been in desperate straits as a Methodist Episcopal affiliated college in Beaver, Pa. Its enrollments had declined, it was on the verge of bankruptcy, unable to pay its creditors, and the University Senate of the Methodist Episcopal Church, the Church's accrediting agency for its affiliated colleges, had withdrawn recognition of the College as an institution capable of awarding bachelor's degrees. Dr. Matthew H. Reaser, President of the Beechwood School in Jenkintown, Pennsylvania, appeared from nowhere, an apparent savior of the collapsing College. Dr. Lynn Harris, President of Beaver College at the time, reports that, while he had several lines of inquiry out about possible mergers, he was not sure how Dr. Reaser was directed to his attention. He states that, "Dr. Reaser had it in mind that he could buy the college charter and thus enhance the money-making value of his school. I convinced him that such a deal was impossible, and that, for matters to be legal, the college would have to purchase Beechwood. (. . . I had an idea even then that the Presbyterian church might be led to adopt the college, in view of the fund shortly, under the will of—I can't recall the name—to be given to a college in or near his 'beloved Philadelphia' . . .)."

While no substantiating documentation exists, it is clear that Dr. Reaser knew of the Curran estate left to a Presbyterian woman's college in the vicinity of Philadelphia. Before founding Beechwood School, Dr. Reaser served as President of Wilson College, located in Chambersburg, Pennsylvania. Reverend Tryon Edwards, D. D., a close friend and collaborator of Dr. Curran, had been Chairman of the Board of Trustees of Wilson College and was thoroughly familiar with Dr. Curran's will. Because a college meeting the criteria of Curran's will did not exist, Dr. Reaser may have sought to secure the legacy for his own purposes by merging the two schools. There now would be a women's college adjacent to Philadelphia. The mortgage Beaver College used to purchase Beechwood School would provide Dr. Reaser with a sizable income for the rest of his life. He would not be directly involved in running the College, but his interests would be protected by having three of the new seven-member Board of Trustees consist of men loyal to him, one of whom, his son-in-law Mr. Shannon C. Wallace, also served as Business Manager and Treasurer of the merged institution. If the College could win the Curran Fund, it would strengthen the economic viability of the new institution and further secure Dr. Reaser's income. Of course, Wilson College also knew of the Curran legacy.

Dr. Harris was sure enough of the possibility that Beaver College could qualify for the Curran estate that, on June 19, 1925, before the College left Beaver. Pa., he presented a resolution to the Board of Trustees suggesting that they send a letter "to the Committee in charge of the assignment of income of the Curran Fund in the city of Philadelphia," stating the College's interest in the Fund. A year later, at the Board of Trustees meeting on May 29, 1926, in Jenkintown, he recommended to the Board that, "the President of the Board be empowered to offer the court, or other proper authority, to meet, on behalf of the Corporation, any conditions that may be laid down by said court, or other proper authority, in order for Beaver College to obtain the benefits of this Fund." What Dr. Harris, a Methodist, did not anticipate was that, at the same meeting, in order to make way for a Presbyterian president, the Board passed the following resolution, "Whereas there is a probability that the church affiliation of the President of Beaver College may be of very great importance to the institution's future. Be it resolved that notice is hereby given to Dr. Lynn H. Harris that his services may not be required after the close of the scholastic year in June 1927." The notice was later rescinded to allow President Harris to resign of his own free will effective September 1, 1927. The Board, in recognition of his services, awarded him $1,500 (half of his annual salary). Dr. Jesse Penny Martin was named Acting President until the selection of a new president.

In fact, the Board of Trustees was orchestrating a deliberate plan to qualify for the proceeds of the Curran estate. At the May 28, 1927 Board meeting, Dr. Reaser reported on the Curran Fund stating that Beaver College "had the best chance of any institution seeking the same." Obviously Beaver College was a women's college located adjacent to Philadelphia, but it moved from Beaver to Jenkintown as a nonsectarian college. It could qualify for the Curran estate only if it became a Presbyterian affiliated college.

At the December 12, 1927 meeting of the Board of Trustees, Trustees Richardson and Darragh recommended Dr. Walter B. Greenway for the "presidency of the College as soon as his services may be available at a salary of Ten Thousand ($10,000) Dollars per year, and on a three to five year contract." Dr. Greenway was a prominent and influential Presbyterian minister who at one time was moderator of the Philadelphia Presbytery. When he received the call to become President of Beaver College he was pastor of the Bethany Temple Presbyterian Church, the second-largest and one of the wealthiest congregations in Philadelphia. The *Philadelphia Inquirer* of March 16, 1928 announced that Dr. Greenway had been elected President of Beaver College, but that he would not announce his decision until after Easter. The same article went on to state, "Dr. Greenway is chairman of the special committee of the Presbytery of Philadelphia to take care of the interests of the body with reference to the disposal of the estate of the late Dr. William Curran, now valued at more than $1,250,000. According to the will of Dr. Curran, the income from the estate, which last year was more than $82,000, is to be used for the Christian education of young women "in or near Philadelphia" and is to be under the supervision of the Presbyterian Church . . . . It is understood that Dr. Greenway has been strongly in favor of Beaver College securing the bulk of the Curran endowment." The $10,000 salary he was offered as president was over three times that of his predecessor, Dr. Harris.

Dr. Greenway verbally accepted the presidency of Beaver College at the March 29, 1928 meeting of the Board of Trustees. Later, in a number of forums, Dr. Greenway stated that he accepted the presidency only under the condition that Beaver College would become affiliated with the Presbyterian Church. However, there is nothing in his contract or in the minutes of the Board to substantiate this assertion. Later, in the same meeting, the Board voted "to enlarge the membership of the Board of Trustees, and to provide that two-thirds of the

Dr. Jesse Penny Martin, Acting President (1927–1928). (Arcadia University Archives)

Dr. Walter Burton Greenway, President (1928–1939). (Arcadia University Archives) membership of such ultimate Board, shall be members of the Presbyterian Church to meet the requirements of the Curran will, which requires the supervision of the Presbyterian Church of the United States of America and to meet any other reasonable requirements."

The Board of Trustees, at meetings on June 20 and July 13, 1928, crafted a set of amendments to the College's charter establishing the College's domicile in Montgomery County, Pennsylvania, and its relationship to the Presbyterian Church. The latter amendments stated, "the Board of Trustees of Beaver College shall consist of not more than 18 persons, two-thirds of whom shall always be members in good standing in the Presbyterian Church . . . ," and that "Beaver College shall always maintain a connection with the Presbyterian Church, USA and that if at any time all connection with the Presbyterian Church, USA should be severed by act of Beaver College, the cash amount of all endowments, principals, or gift invested in real estate, received from Presbyterian sources shall be turned over in the original amounts to the Board of Christian Education of the Presbyterian Church."

On August 16, 1928, the Board of Trustees petitioned the Beaver County Court to amend its charter so that it could become affiliated with the Presbyterian Church. A headline in *The Daily Times*, Beaver, Pa., stated, "Presbyterians will take over Beaver College." The article went on to say, "Indications that it will separate from the Methodist church with which it has been affiliated since its organization were evidenced today when the board of directors of Beaver College presented a petition to the Beaver county courts, amending the charter to be under the wing of the Presbyterian church." The Court granted the amendments at a hearing on September 1, 1928.

Even before the Beaver County Court approved the amendments, the Trustees acted to strengthen the Board's Presbyterian character. Two prominent Presbyterian Elders were appointed to the Board. Allen Sutherland, President of the Erie National Bank and a Director of the Presbyterian Board of Christian Education was elected President of the Board. J. M. Steele, President of the Philadelphia Y.M.C.A., Treasurer of the Presbyterian Church's Foreign Mission Board, and Covenanter of the Presbyterian Church, joined him on the Board. Other prominent Presbyterian ministers and laymen subsequently were added to the Board.

The Board meeting of September 22, 1928 had a full agenda. A committee of Trustees was appointed to make Beaver College known to the ministers of the Synod of Pennsylvania, important because the Synod's ministers eventually would vote on the College's application to become a Presbyterian related college. A second committee was appointed "to apply to the Synod of the Presbyterian Church, USA for recognition of Beaver College as a Presbyterian school." The Bylaws of the Board of Trustees were amended to give the Synod the right of approval on the election of all Board members. Finally, the Board moved to "petition the Orphan's Court of Philadelphia to grant to Beaver College the income from the Dr. William Curran estate as qualifying in all ways under the Will."

The Synod of Pennsylvania at its annual meeting on October 16, 1928 accepted Beaver College as a Presbyterian College, "on condition that two-thirds of the Trustees shall always be members of the Presbyterian Church and the Synod shall have the Power of veto or approval of all Trustees." Beaver College was now a Presbyterian affiliated college, but to strengthen its position even further, the trustees applied to the national Board of Christian Education of the Presbyterian Church, for recognition of the College as a Presbyterian institution. After several visits to the College, the Board of Christian Education "Received Beaver College as one of the family of Presbyterian Colleges with which it cooperates."

As the Curran estate had reached the financial goals set by Dr. Curran in his will, the Fidelity-Philadelphia Trust Company petitioned the Orphan's Court of Philadelphia on September 22, 1929 to allow it to begin distributing the income from the estate. A hearing was held before Judge John M. Gest to determine how the income should be distributed. During the hearing, the Vice President of the Fidelity-Philadelphia Trust Company testified and recommended that the income from the estate should be awarded to Wilson College, a Presbyterian institution in Chambersburg, Pennsylvania. He stated that his opinion was based on the recommendation of the majority of the Committee of Twelve and also on that of the President of the Trust Company, William P. Gest. Judge Gest then stated that he was William P. Gest's brother and would be embarrassed in giving a decision that concurred with or dissented from the opinion of his brother. He recused himself from the hearing and on December 28, 1929, appointed Francis P. Biddle of the Philadelphia Bar as Master in the case. The Master's task was to audit the estate, hold hearings, gather facts, and make recommendations to the Orphan's Court as to the proper distribution of the Curran legacy.

There were three claimants for the Curran Fund: Beaver College, Philadelphia School for Christian Workers, and Wilson College. Hearings were held in Biddle's offices from January 21, 1930 through April 25, 1930. Each school called witnesses and presented evidence as to why it should be awarded the income from the Curran estate. During May, Mr. Biddle personally visited each of the three institutions. He filed his report in the Orphan's Court on October 31, 1930. Philadelphia School for Christian Workers, although a Presbyterian school located in Philadelphia, was immediately eliminated from consideration because it was not a college and was not an exclusively female institution. In the Master's opinion, the contest was between Beaver College and Wilson College.

In comparing the two institutions, Biddle's report made clear that Wilson College was academically superior to Beaver College. Wilson College was accredited by Middle States and approved by the American Association of University Women, while Beaver College was not recognized by any accrediting body. Wilson College had an endowment of $708,000 with no debt; Beaver College had no endowment and massive debt. Wilson College's library had 23,000 volumes, Beaver College's 10,000. Wilson College had 47 full-time faculty of whom 14 held the Ph.D. and 22 the M.A.; Beaver College had 48 full-time faculty of whom only

7 held the Ph.D. and 7 a M.A. A comparison of salaries showed Wilson College's faculty to be significantly better paid. Almost all of Wilson College's students were enrolled in liberal arts programs, while 92% of Beaver College's students were enrolled in vocationally oriented programs, with the largest number receiving a B.S. in Education. All freshman at Wilson were required to study Latin and many were enrolled in Greek and advanced courses in these two languages, whereas Beaver College did not require any ancient language and had much smaller numbers of students enrolled in such courses. Both institutions did require courses in the Bible. Biddle, in describing the education received at Beaver College said, "A good deal of this instruction is elementary, some superficial. The type of instruction is not comparable to that given at Wilson."

However, the Master reasoned, "The testator intended to benefit a college in or adjacent to Philadelphia. Wilson is not such a college . . . . Beaver is a college for young women adjacent to Philadelphia. It thus fulfills what the auditor [Master] considers the dominant purpose of the testator. It seems, therefore, of little importance to the auditor that Beaver College may be poorly financed, if it can do what is required . . . . That Beaver cannot compare to Wilson in scholastic standing is immaterial; nor is it important in making our choice that the members of the Beaver faculty may be underpaid." Biddle's recommendations for the disbursal of the annual income from the estate included not only the scholarships for female students, but also that portions of the annual income be used to strengthen the College's library holdings, increase the salaries of its teachers, and establish an endowment.

The Main Hall, Wilson College, Chambersburg, Pa., circa 1931. (Photos courtesy of the C. Elizabeth Boyd '33 Archives, Wilson College)

Mr. Biddle filed his report with the Orphan's Court on October 31, 1930. The Orphan's Court was not impressed by the Master's reasoning and on June 5, 1931, declined the report and recommitted it to Biddle asking him to take further testimony particularly "as will throw more light on the academic and financial status of Beaver College." The supplemental report that Mr. Biddle eventually filed (on April 27, 1932) merely reiterated the facts and conclusions of his earlier report. Biddle still recommended that Beaver College be the recipient of the Curran estate.

On June 17, 1932, the Orphan's Court considered its Master's report. The Court sat "in banc," all five of the Court's judges participating in the hearing. The opinion written for the Court by Judge Henderson states, "Both claimants admit that the education directed by

Main Book Room of Wilson
College's John Stewart
Memorial Library, circa 1931.
(Photo courtesy of the
C. Elizabeth Boyd '33
Archives, Wilson College)

Main Book Room of
Beaver College's Library
in Huntington Hall. (Arcadia
University Archives)

the Will should be: higher classical, highly cultural, with emphasis on Biblical teaching and a missionary spirit . . . . Beyond all question Wilson easily qualifies under all of these three heads . . . . We are of the opinion that Beaver utterly fails in these qualifications . . . . We are of the opinion that the Auditor [the Master] fell into error when he recommended that all of the essentials of Dr. Curran's plan were to be sacrificed in order that the institution should be in the Philadelphia neighborhood. Education such as this will specifies is a much more important thing than mere location . . . ." The Court awarded the income from the Curran estate to Wilson College, 140 miles distant from Philadelphia.

A special meeting of Beaver College's Board of Trustees was held on July 25, 1932. Ralph B. Evans, one of the College's lawyers, reviewed the Orphan Court's decision and said that the only remaining option for the Board was to appeal the Orphan Court's decision to the Pennsylvania State Supreme Court. He estimated that the College had an "even chance" of reversing the Orphans' Court's decision. After discussion, the Board unanimously voted to appeal the decision.

On March 13, 1933, the State Supreme Court heard the appeal of Beaver College. After reviewing the earlier court decisions, the Court agreed with the Orphan's Court ruling that the Master erred in placing location above quality. In addition, the Supreme Court felt that, "The rapid advances which have taken place in modes of transportation and communication since Dr. Curran's death in 1880 has altered the conception of the distance between places. The advent of the telephone and airplane, motorcars and paved roads, as well as faster and more frequent rail service, has greatly lessened the time required for all journeys. A trip from Chambersburg to Philadelphia is no more arduous at the present time than travel to the city from outlying districts at the time the will was written. Under the standards applicable in the lifetime of testator, Chambersburg may at present readily be considered 'adjacent' to Philadelphia in considering and determining the question now before us."

Thus ended Beaver College's pursuit of the Curran legacy. The pot of gold in the vicinity of Philadelphia proved to be as elusive as the proverbial pot of gold at the end of the rainbow.

Sources

Decree in the Orphan's Court of Philadelphia County on the Estate of William Curran, Deceased, June 5, 1931, recommitting the Master's report.

Decree in the Orphan's Court of Philadelphia County on the Estate of William Curran, Deceased, June 17, 1932.

Decree of the Supreme Court of Pennsylvania on the appeal of Beaver College, No. 346, January Term, 1932, May 14–15, 1933.

Dr. Walter Greenway Elected Beaver Head. *Philadelphia Inquirer*, Philadelphia, Pa., March 16, 1928.

Letter from Dr. Lynn Harris to Dean Ruth L. Higgins, May 22, 1953.

Minutes of the Beaver College Board of Trustees, 1925–1932.

Minutes, 1928, Synod of Pennsylvania, Presbyterian Church in the United States of America, Grove City, Pa., October 16, 1928.

Presbyterians Will Take Over Beaver College. *The Daily Times*, Beaver, Pa., August 6, 1928.

Report of F. B. Biddle, Auditor on the Estate of William Curran, Deceased, to the Orphan's Court of Philadelphia County, October 31, 1930

Supplemental Report of F. B. Biddle, Auditor on the Estate of William Curran, Deceased, to the Orphan's Court of Philadelphia County, April 27, 1932.

Will of William Curran, probated before the Register of Wills at Philadelphia in 1883 and recorded in will book 120, page 399.

JENKINTOWN AND GLENSIDE, PA.

A PHOTO ESSAY

An artist's rendering of a composite view of the two campuses of Beaver College. The Jenkintown campus is pictured in the foreground; the Glenside campus is in the background. The main buildings shown on the Jenkintown campus are, left to right: Beaver Hall, Taylor Hall and Chapel, Huntington Hall (library and gymnasium), and Montgomery Hall. Ivy Hall (student residence and swimming pool) is located behind Beaver Hall on the left. The second white house behind Montgomery Hall is Florence Lodge, the President's House. The main buildings portrayed on the Glenside campus are, left to right: Murphy Hall, Grey Towers, Brookside Hall (now the Spruance Art Center and Little Theatre), and the Gate House (now Blake Hall). (Laurel Art Co., Cheltenham, Pa., Arcadia University Archives)

The gatehouse on the Glenside campus over the years was variously named The Lodge, The French House, The Gate House, and, currently, Blake Hall. Initially used as a student residence, the building subsequently has housed the Music Department, student clubs and organizations, College Relations Offices, and, at the present time, University Development offices. (Photo by Harry Utzy, Jenkintown, Pa.; Arcadia University Archives)

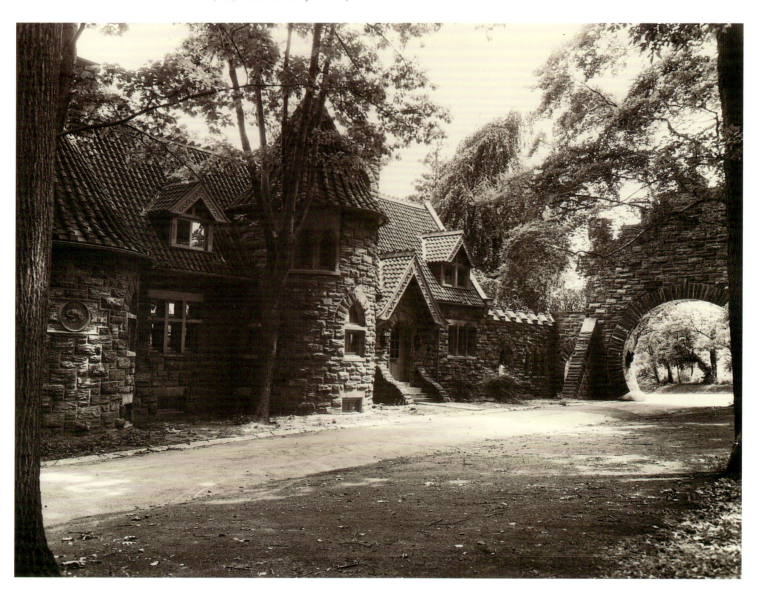

Murphy Hall, originally the carriage house of the estate, was used for science labs, a gymnasium, and faculty offices. The area above the gymnasium (currently Stitler Auditorium) was used as the Chapel. (Arcadia University Archives)

The gymnasium located in Murphy Hall on the Glenside campus circa 1930. This area is now offices and instructional space for Music, Communications, and Fine Arts. (Photo by Richard T. Dooner, Philadelphia, Pa.; Arcadia University Archives)

The well of the Harrison estate, which originally had a thatched roof, still stands by the Dining Hall Complex. It now has a shingle roof and houses the bell (a gift of the Class of 1938) that once hung outside of Taylor Chapel on the Jenkintown campus. (Photo by A. Jackson Co., Baltimore, Md.; Arcadia University Archives)

A duck pond (Alnwick Pool) once existed at the bottom of the hill behind Grey Towers Castle where Brubaker Hall now stands. The pond was destroyed when the stream that fed the pond was dammed by the construction of the Route 309 Expressway in the spring of 1959. (Arcadia University Archives)

Students enjoying a snack in a Beaver Hall room. Students sitting on beds from left to right are Doris Pratt '47, Beverly Peterson '49, and Pauline Cadwallader '49; those sitting on floor from left to right are Daphne Gamsby and Carol Kunz '49. (Arcadia University Archives)

Two students working on biology laboratory exercises in Murphy Hall. The student on the right is dissecting a sand shark. (Photo by Harry J. Utzy, Jenkintown, Pa.; Arcadia University Archives)

Montgomery Hall residence on the Jenkintown campus. (Arcadia University Archives)

Student athletics in the 1930s–1940s.

Jimmy D'Angelo, Baederwood Golf Club pro, provides golf instruction to students on the Glenside campus. (Photo by Harry Utzy, Jenkintown, Pa.; Arcadia University Archives)

Field hockey game circa 1940. (Arcadia University Archives)

Swimming in the indoor pool in the basement of Ivy Hall on the Jenkintown campus. (Photo by Alquist Studio, Jenkintown, Pa.; Arcadia University Archives)

Dr. W. Lawrence Curry, Professor of Music (1929–1966) and Chair of the Department, with the Glee Club in Murphy Hall Chapel (later Stitler Auditorium) circa 1953. Dr. Curry conducted the Glee Club from 1936 to 1959. (Arcadia University Archives)

FROM FEMALE SEMINARY TO COMPREHENSIVE UNIVERSITY [15]

PART IV: THE EVOLUTION OF THE UNIVERSITY 1954–2003

Mark P. Curchack

The second half of the twentieth century was a time of unprecedented growth in higher education across the United States, with overall expansion of educational opportunity, ongoing academic innovation, and occasional moments of turmoil. Beaver College partook of all those trends, and led the way in some. The University which emerged was heir to the many proud accomplishments of its past.

[15] Portions of this essay have been adapted from an unpublished, 1980 manuscript covering the years from 1954 to 1979 entitled "Beaver College" written by Dean Margaret F. LeClair. A shorter version of that manuscript was printed in J.B. Toll & M.J. Schwager (Eds.). *Montgomery County: The second hundred years*, (Vol. 2, pp. 1112–1114). Norristown, Pa.,: Montgomery County Federation of Historical Societies. Both works are used by permission.

Four Arcadia University students descend the "Alumni Walk of Pride," a beautiful promenade dedicated to alumni who have made the Arcadia Alumni Fund a philanthropic priority in their lives. Students pictured are (from left to right): Matthew Melcher '02, Sarah Engelstad '03, Christina Barth '03, and Charles (C.J.) Maschi '03. (Photo by Brian Ferreira, Haddon Heights, N.J.; Arcadia University Archives)

THE EVOLUTION OF
THE UNIVERSITY 1954–2003

The years following the Centennial saw the growth of a more selective and more highly regarded college for women. Beaver's enrollment climbed from 325 in 1925 to 678 full-time students the decade after the merger, suffered a decline during the war years, but underwent a strong resurgence during the 1950s.

THE 1960s: CAMPUS CONSOLIDATION AND FACILITIES DEVELOPMENT

A New Campus Is Built

By the mid-1950s, even with the addition of a small residence hall built on the Glenside campus, Thomas Hall, Beaver could not accept all the qualified applicants who wished to enroll. Students also came from a much wider geographical range. Crowding was being felt in the library and in other student service areas on the main, Jenkintown site.

When the fall semester opened in 1960, the problems of housing the library and infirmary had not been resolved, but by 1961 the Eugenia Fuller Atwood Library, named for its donor, was under construction, and in the spring of 1962, the Ruck Health Center, a gift of George D. Ruck, opened, both on the Glenside campus.

The Trustees had previously determined that the long-delayed complete consolidation on the Harrison estate in Glenside should go forward with dispatch. Board discussion about such a move intensified as the 1950s wore on. As the decade drew to a close, blueprints for three new residence halls, a dining hall, and a classroom building were nearing completion.

In early November 1960, groundbreaking ceremonies took place for the federally-funded dormitory-dining hall complex. Within less than two years, eight new buildings and extensive renovations to Grey Towers had been completed, and the College moved all of its operations to Glenside in June 1962. The entire consolidation process cost roughly $4,130,000 (over $25,000,000 in 2002 dollars). The College borrowed heavily to meet these expenses with the largest single loan in the form of $2,100,000 in Federal bonds, the rest privately donated or borrowed; it also counted on funds from the sale of the Jenkintown campus. That sale encountered complications, however, and was not finalized until 1964.

Facilities extension in the remaining years of the decade included remodeling of and additions to the Little

Thomas Hall, named after
long-time Trustee and College
benefactor, Morgan Thomas,
was opened in 1955.
(Arcadia University Archives)

Eugenia Fuller Atwood Library,
named for long-time Trustee,
Vice President of the Board
of Trustees, and College
benefactor, was completed
in 1962. At the time it was
an ideal example of a small
college library. (Arcadia
University Archives)

Mrs. Eugenia Fuller Atwood,
member of the Board of
Trustees (1957–1966), and
Vice President of the Board
(1960–1966), and her husband,
Mr. John C. Atwood, Jr., laid
the cornerstone of the Atwood
Library at its dedication on
April 29, 1962. The cornerstone
contained a time capsule
that will be opened during the
University's Sesquicentennial
Celebration. (Photo by Jules
Schick, Philadelphia, Pa.;
Arcadia University Archives)

President Edward D. Gates explaining to a student leader the plans to consolidate the College on the Glenside campus. The picture was taken in his office in Beaver Hall on the Jenkintown campus. (Arcadia University Archives)

An aerial view of Beaver College in Glenside in 1962. Clockwise from Grey Towers Castle, the buildings are: Ruck Health Center, Murphy Hall, the Art Studio and Little Theatre complex, the Classroom Building (later Taylor Hall), Atwood Library, Heinz Hall, and the dining and residence complex (Dilworth, Thomas, and Kistler Halls). Blake Hall is among the trees to the right of Heinz Hall. The outdoor swimming pool can be seen between Murphy Hall and the Art Studio complex (later Spruance Art Center), the field hockey field to the left of the Classroom Building, and the tennis courts below the Classroom Building and Atwood Library. (Arcadia University Archives)

Administrative Changes with Lasting Effects

Theatre (1966) and the Benton Spruance Art Center (1969), largely through gifts from Mr. and Mrs. John C. Atwood, Jr. Careful restoration of the Rose and Mirror Rooms in Grey Towers (1969) was accomplished through the generosity of Marion Angell Boyer.

At the end of 1959–60, President Kistler and Dean Higgins retired. To succeed them, the Board appointed Dr. Edward D. Gates, General Secretary of Macalester College, and Dr. Margaret F. LeClair, Dean of Margaret Morrison Carnegie College, Carnegie-Mellon University. Both would spend two decades at the institution. The rapid recovery in enrollment after 1945 was overseen by Miss Marjorie Darling, Director of Admissions from 1943 to 1972 and Dean of Admissions, 1972–73. In 1969, a new registrar arrived on campus. Mr. Harold (Hal) Stewart has served in that capacity up to the time of this publication, a period of almost unimaginable change in the processes of keeping student records.

During most of the 1960s, and beyond, the Board of Trustees, chaired by John W. Cornell, Jr., president of the oldest building firm in Philadelphia, gave generously of time and effort as well as funds. Among the most actively involved Trustees, in addition to Mrs. Atwood and Mr. Ruck, were Ira R. Kraybill, Vira I. Heinz, Wilmot E. Fleming (later state senator), Harold W. Scott, Harry G. Kuch, John V. Calhoun, Sr., and John A. Mitchell.

Academic Developments in the Sixties

Once the consolidation in Glenside had been accomplished, an Educational Policy Committee undertook an intensive review of the academic program. Two major challenges confronted the committee: 1) under-enrollment in several professional programs and liberal arts majors, resulting in the proliferation of courses and very small classes; and 2) the lack of a statement of academic goals and objectives encompassing the entire academic program.

Although Beaver called itself a liberal arts college, it had almost from the beginning offered programs that did not traditionally fall into that category. Indeed, both Beechwood and Beaver made a point of the "practical" along with the "cultural," and Liberal Arts (under various labels through the years) was listed as a separate curriculum. According to the 1954–55 catalog, "professional" curricula included Business Administration, Kindergarten-Elementary Education, Fine Arts, Health and Physical Education, Home Economics, Music, and Medical Technology. Some of these curricula offered several concentrations; for example, under Business Administration were Management, Administrative Secretarial, and Retailing; under Home Economics were General, Education, and Dietetics. Moreover, while a liberal arts requirement was a component of each curriculum, these courses were often specialized in terms of the particular program; e.g., General Science for Elementary Education or Nutrition; Applied Psychology for Business.

Mr. Harry G. Kuch, member
of the Board of Trustees
(1947–1993) and major College
benefactor. The Kuch Athletic
and Recreation Center is
named after Dr. Kuch and his
wife, Catherine, in recognition
of the major gift they gave
towards its construction.
(Arcadia University Archives)

Dr. Adeline Gomberg, Professor of Education (1961–1981), and an education major work with children from Fitler Elementary School, Philadelphia, Pa., in the Reading Clinic located on the third floor of the Classroom Building. (Arcadia University Archives)

The Classroom Building opened in 1962. In addition to classrooms and faculty offices, the building also housed the offices of Academic Affairs, Registrar, Student Affairs, and, later, the Graduate Office. The Office of Student Affairs is now in Knight Hall. In 1995 the classroom building was named Taylor Hall in honor of the third President of Beaver College. (Arcadia University Archives)

Heinz Hall, opened in 1962, was named in honor of Mrs. Vira Heinz, long-term member of the Board of Trustees and major College benefactor. Pictured is a typical residence room in Heinz Hall in the late 1960s. The students are freshmen Carolyn Walker and Louise Wagner '73. (Arcadia University Archives)

A sociology student interviews a client in a nursing home as part of her casework internship. (Arcadia University Archives)

Under the most favorable circumstances, such a multiplicity of curricula would strain the resources of a college with only 600 students. After World War II, the young women who chose to attend an Eastern women's college became less and less interested in immediate employment upon graduation. Many liberal arts colleges which had introduced vocationally-oriented programs in the thirties were phasing them out in the fifties. At Beaver, Elementary Education and Fine Arts continued to flourish, but enrollment in the other professional programs diminished drastically, resulting in high costs per student and fragmentation of faculty efforts in the traditional liberal arts areas where students were concentrating.

When the Educational Policy Committee began its study of the academic program, the Bachelor of Music and the B.S. in Home Economics had already been discontinued. Revisions that followed were the phasing out of Business Administration, Health and Physical Education, and Fashion Design. Course offerings in all areas were pruned, as were major programs that attracted few students; for example, Classical Languages, American Civilization, and several of the more applied areas in Fine Arts.

Meanwhile, the Educational Policy Committee was seeking to define a viable concept of liberal education and to formulate a statement of all-College goals to guide the future development of the academic program. The resulting document was adopted by the Faculty and the

Board of Trustees in 1963. The goals of the undergraduate program as stated therein remained essentially unchanged until the advent of sustained long-range and strategic planning in the late 1980s.

> The academic program is designed to help students acquire 1) basic information and concepts about man, nature, and society; 2) specialization of some depth in a field of their choice as a basis for career opportunities, graduate study, a profession, or their own satisfaction; 3) intellectual abilities needed for continued learning and the creative use of knowledge throughout life.

A sequential core of required courses (1965) responded to the first goal. The second goal indicated that Beaver had not abandoned career education, and programs increasingly emphasized experience in the field. Student teaching was extended and practicum experience added to most Education courses. A reading clinic for disadvantaged pupils was established in cooperation with the Philadelphia School District (1965). Psychology, Sociology, Political Science, and the Natural Sciences either required or provided optional on-the-job experience in their major programs. Beaver was, in fact, among the first of the liberal arts colleges to arrange apprenticeships in areas other than teacher education.

The third goal meant encouraging students to discover knowledge on their own and providing constant practice in the use of intellectual skills broadly applicable

111

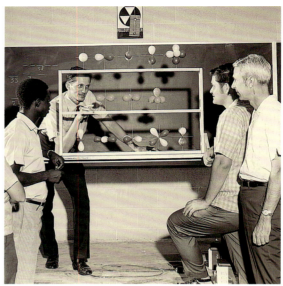

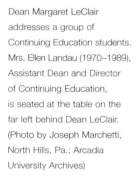

Dean Margaret LeClair addresses a group of Continuing Education students. Mrs. Ellen Landau (1970–1989), Assistant Dean and Director of Continuing Education, is seated at the table on the far left behind Dean LeClair. (Photo by Joseph Marchetti, North Hills, Pa.; Arcadia University Archives)

Dr. Arthur C. Breyer (1964–1992), Professor of Chemistry and Chair of the Department of Chemistry and Physics, demonstrates a device for teaching atomic structure to high school chemistry teachers participating in one of his National Science Foundation-funded Summer Institutes in Chemistry. (Photo by ATOModels, Willow Grove, Pa.; Arcadia University Archives)

to all areas of human endeavor. The essence of liberal education was thus defined as helping students acquire the habits of inquiry and judicious thought needed for continuing self-education and the resourcefulness to deal with the ambiguities and problems of a world characterized by swift change. In order to promote intellectual excellence among their students, the faculty developed and approved an Honors Program in 1967 (it was initiated in the 1968–69 year). A pass-fail option, adopted in 1969, permitted students to broaden their educational experience and to experiment with new subject areas.

In the early 1960s, the Board of Christian Education of the United Presbyterian Church in the U.S.A. liberalized the guidelines for its related colleges. Religious affiliation was no longer a consideration in appointment of faculty, and chapel services became optional. The former change led to a considerable diversification among the faculty and, in the opinions of many, an overall enhancement in the background achievements of the new faculty hired in that decade. References to evangelical Christianity in former catalogs were replaced by a statement that, as a church-related college, Beaver emphasized Judeo-Christian ideals as part of the national heritage.

Other significant developments in the sixties saw the College reach out to the community and step out on the national and, indeed, international stage. In 1961 Beaver became the first college in the Philadelphia area to admit adult women on a part-time basis to degree

programs in which they attended regular day classes along with undergraduates of the traditional college age, this at a time before community colleges emerged to offer similar opportunities to adult students.

Over the next two decades, this group of Continuing Education students (as they were called) formed a meaningful part of each year's enrollment. Summer institutes for high school chemistry teachers funded by the National Science Foundation began in 1965, under the direction of Dr. Arthur Breyer of the Chemistry Department. The following year the Faculty approved granting credit for off-campus work-study semesters in urban centers such as Philadelphia, Harrisburg, and Washington, D.C. Several years later (1972), Dr. Samuel Cameron instituted a long-running summer program for high school teachers in psychology.

Beaver College formally created its Center for Education Abroad (CEA) in 1965. As the accompanying essay on the history of CEA shows (see pp. 164–171), the College had been sending students to Europe for nearly twenty years. The initial CEA program was a London Semester, but new opportunities soon appeared. CEA's founding Director, Dr. David Gray, conceived a plan to have CEA serve as a conduit for overseas study, primarily in the British Isles, by students from other colleges and universities in the U.S. In later years, Dr. Gray would be given the title of Vice President and would go on to manage other projects on behalf of the institution, among them

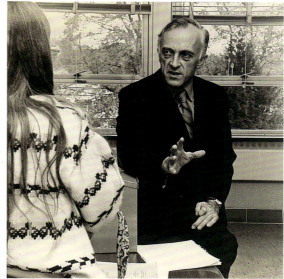

the creation of the January Winterim mini-semester and the change to coeducation.

The plan to open CEA to the nation achieved unexpected success, and by the late 1970s, CEA had become one of the country's largest and most respected study abroad operations. The surplus income from the CEA operation, with enrollments of about 1,500 students annually, supported an increasingly struggling Glenside campus budget. As CEA grew, however, and looked almost exclusively outside for its enrollment, it grew estranged from the day-to-day life of the College. This relationship would not be restored until the 1990s.

Through President Gates's and Dean LeClair's leadership, faculty salaries increased substantially during the 1960s. Teaching loads were reduced to the national norm of twelve lecture/recitation hours. Highly creative persons joined the faculty, whose imagination and cooperation made possible the developments previously described. Individual faculty members secured government grants for their own research and matching funds for equipment for the College. Psychology Department Chair, Dr. Bernard Mausner, secured a three-year grant (1968–1971) of approximately a quarter of a million dollars under the National Science Foundation College Science Improvement Program (COSIP) to fund a number of activities in the sciences and social sciences, including the development of an interdisciplinary science course, laboratory instruction in psychology courses, and a self-

paced statistics course. Mrs. Ellen Landau was hired as an assistant under another Psychology Grant, this time to study the educational effectiveness of the Public Broadcasting System's *Sesame Street* television program; she went on to serve as an academic counselor, the Director of Continuing Education, and in a variety of other capacities, ultimately becoming the Assistant Dean of the College until she left the College in 1989.

Although the primary responsibility of the Beaver faculty was teaching, an increasing number began to participate in other professional activities: publishing, presenting papers at meetings of scholarly associations, conducting workshops and conferences, exhibiting art works, performing, recording, and composing music.

Faculty productivity and President Gates's service on state and national educational associations increased the visibility of the College. Its academic reputation, consequently, steadily advanced. Further evidence of this progress was seen in the fact that fundraising in the first five Gates years totaled $1,561,919, compared to $1,425,287 for the entire period 1922 to 1960.

Campus Life in the "Student" Decade

Social activities at Beaver in the sixties bore little resemblance to life under the Taylors in the prior century. Many of the earlier prohibitions gradually disappeared following the move to Jenkintown. From 1925 onward, student government became progressively stronger. When

Dr. Bernard Mausner (1962–1992), Professor of Psychology and Chair of the Department, and psychology students work with a Skinner box in the Boyer Hall psychology laboratory in the mid-1980s. (Arcadia University Archives)

Dr. Norman Johnston (1962–1992), Professor of Sociology and Chair of the Department, answers a question of a student at the end of class in the Classroom Building (Taylor Hall). (Arcadia University Archives)

113

A group of "Freshies" undergoing typical hazing by tipping their beanies to upperclass students during Freshman Week, 1945, on the steps of Beaver Hall on the Jenkintown campus. (Arcadia University Archives)

TRADITIONS OF THE PAST

Beaver College had a number of traditions that brought the College community together and fostered class and college spirit. Many of the traditions were abandoned in the late 1960s and early 1970s when students were more involved in societal issues and such customs seemed quaint and irrelevant. In earlier years, though, the sequence of the traditions marked the rhythm of the social calendar.

Freshmen Beanies

It is not clear when this form of hazing began. All freshmen were required by the upperclassmen to wear a class beanie from the first week of classes until the "freshies" won the right to discard them. The caps were clearly a mark of subservient status; freshmen had to tip their hats whenever directly encountering an upperclass student. In addition, upperclass students had the prerogative of subjecting freshmen to various humiliating pranks. The rationale for the practice was to incorporate the new students into the college community and to create class spirit.

In 1958, the Student Government Association banned all forms of "immature and excess hazing." While the immature pranks were eliminated, the beanie tradition continued. Originally, freshmen were required to wear their caps until late November at Song Contest. Over time, the tradition changed to allow freshmen an earlier opportunity to shed their hats. After classes on a designated day in mid-October, the freshmen serenaded the upperclass students followed by a tug-of-war between the freshmen and the sophomores on the hockey field at 5 p.m. If the freshmen won, they discarded their beanies; if they lost, they had to wear the caps for another month until Song Contest. During Song Contest the upperclass students voted on the freshman class's performance and usually, after some suspenseful teasing, permitted the "freshies" to discard their caps into a large decorated box. The tradition ended in the early 1970s.

A 1970 freshman beanie. (Photo by Jerome Lukowicz, Philadelphia, Pa.; Arcadia University Archives)

Song Contest

This hugely popular tradition started in 1932. It was so much enjoyed and involved so much student energy and time that, in order to maintain academic standards, the faculty had to limit the hours students could spend creating and rehearsing the songs. The evening before Thanksgiving holiday, the show played to a standing-room-only audience consisting of the entire college community and many alumnae. Interest in Song Contest faded in the late sixties; fewer and fewer students participated, and it was discontinued in 1968.

1958 Song Contest in Murphy Gymnasium. (Arcadia University Archives)

Freshmen march gleefully down the aisle of Murphy Gymnasium to shed their beanies following Song Contest. (Photo by Merin Studios, Philadelphia, Pa.; Arcadia University Archives)

Students perform the traditional dance around the May Pole on the Glenside campus lawn during the 1928 May Day pageant. (Arcadia University Archives)

The 1952 Junior Prom Queen and her escort descend the grand stairway of Grey Towers flanked on either side by the Queen's Freshmen Court. The name of the Queen was not announced until during the Prom. (Photo by Merin Studios, Philadelphia, Pa.; Arcadia University Archives)

The senior hoop-rolling contest was a more frivolous tradition of the 1930s and 1940s. Here, seniors from the Class of 1938 compete on the lawn in front of Beaver Hall on the Jenkintown campus. Supposedly, the woman who first rolled her hoop over the line at the bottom of the hill would be the first married. (Arcadia University Archives)

Students sweep and mop the Grey Towers Castle patio and wash windows of the conservatory during Cleanup Day. (Arcadia University Archives)

The silver trowel, used in the Planting of the Ivy Ceremony, was awarded during Senior Week to the junior with the highest academic standing. The recipient used the trowel to plant ivy somewhere on campus. The last student to receive this award was Eileen G. Robinson '68 in 1967. (Photo by Jerome Lukowicz, Philadelphia, Pa.; Arcadia University Archives)

Junior Prom Weekend

This weekend in early April was a grand and elegant affair. It started with a dance with live music on Friday evening. Saturday afternoon there was some sort of entertainment followed by the formal prom in Grey Towers in the evening. The *Beaver News* of Friday, March 13, 1959, for instance, reported that the Junior Prom Weekend planned for April 10–11, would start with a dance on Friday evening with music provided by the Metronomes. Saturday afternoon, Duke Ellington and his band were to play from 2–4 p.m. The formal dance was later that evening with music provided by the Glenn Miller Band.

May Day

May Day, originally held at Beaver College in the middle of the month, but in later years on the first Saturday in May, was a traditional pageant ushering in spring that was celebrated in women's colleges across the country. The earliest known (according to University records) celebration of May Day by Beaver College was in 1884. The pageant was last celebrated at the College in 1968.

It was an elaborate, all-day event that involved months of planning. There was a May Day Queen selected from three candidates: the runner-ups became the Queen's attendants. The procession across the lawn was led by the Laurel Chain (freshmen and sophomores) and the Honor Court (juniors and seniors), made up of five women from each class chosen for scholastic achievement and five chosen from each class for distinction as class leaders. They were followed by the May Day Queen escorted by her attendants, through an aisle formed by the Laurel Chain and Honor Court. Upon arriving at her throne, she was formally crowned by the May Day Queen of the previous year. The Queen then assumed her throne and an elaborate pageant began including the traditional dance around the May Pole. Events later in the afternoon involved parents and family. The day ended with a dance in Grey Towers Castle.

Cleanup Day

Cleanup Day was held in the spring. Classes were dismissed for the day. Students, faculty, administration and staff all donned old clothes and armed with mops, pails, dust cloths, trash bags and rakes they set out to beautify the campus. The tradition was held during the forties and fifties.

Senior Week

A number of events were held during Senior Week following the end of final examinations. The week culminated with Baccalaureate services and Commencement. Among the activities were: Planting of the Ivy, the hoop-rolling contest, the lantern procession, and a father-daughter dance. *Samuel M. Cameron*

Members of the Castleaires, a select College vocal ensemble, rehearse around the piano in 1970. (Arcadia University Archives)

Mrs. Melissa Brown Plummer, Dean of Students (1953–1972). (Photo by Merin Studios, Philadelphia, Pa.; Arcadia University Archives)

Florence M. Brown (later Mrs. Lawrence Plummer) came to the campus in 1953 as Dean of Students, there was still some regulation of students' comings and goings, but curfews were set later and later.

The earlier ban on dancing and the idea of chaperoned dates seemed outdated customs. Under student pressure, the regulation of visiting hours for men in the residence halls was steadily liberalized until regulation was eliminated entirely in 1969. By the time of Dean Plummer's retirement in 1972, students made and enforced their own social regulations through the Student Government Organization, except for certain security measures. Although Junior Proms in the grand manner were discarded in the sixties, discos, coffee houses, and informal dances offered entertainment and relaxation.

Other cultural diversions at Beaver from 1925 through the 1960s, however, would doubtless have found favor in the sight of the founding fathers: the tradition of bringing distinguished lecturers and performers to the campus continued by the Forum program; concerts by the Glee Club, the Amado String Quartet (artists in residence), and the Castleaires, a popular *a cappella* singing ensemble; productions of Theatre Playshop, successor to Beclex (Beaver College Expression Club); and programs sponsored by department clubs and by chapters of national honorary societies. The *Beaver News* (later *The Tower*), the *Log* (the yearbook), and the *Gargoyle*, a literary and art magazine, were midcentury descendants of a series of similar publications under different names. Art exhibits and film series were featured. Intramural and varsity sports emphasized tennis, field hockey, lacrosse, basketball, soccer, softball and equestrian competition.

Beaver College was noted for having a small but high quality major in Physical Education in the 1950s and 1960s, which resulted in regular successes in intercollegiate athletics. Field hockey, basketball, and lacrosse were the most competitive sports, as played against Temple, Ursinus, West Chester, St. Joseph's and the University of Pennsylvania, as well as other smaller institutions. Women's athletic programs in those days were run on a "Play Day" mentality: the "girls" would get together to practice once or twice and then they would play against another school, having perhaps six to ten games per season. Since this was also the case at the other schools, Beaver teams were able to hold their own against all opponents. The discontinuation of the Physical Education major in 1965 caused much upset among its former majors and athletic stars.

Parents' Weekend and Dads' Weekend became traditional events which faculty, students, and their families shared. In 1965, Frances H. Lewis '39 organized the Circle of Beaver Parents, an important means of informing parents about the College and a forum for discussion of parental concerns and suggestions. Miss Lewis, at that time Director of College Relations, subsequently became Vice President for Development and College Relations.

The 1955 undefeated
field hockey team. Three
All-Americans were on the
team. Rosemary Deniken '57
(far right) was selected for
the First Team, Barbara
Heylman '58 (second from left)
and Maxine Swift '58
(fourth from left) were selected
for the Reserve Team.
(Arcadia University Archives)

The 1957 undefeated
basketball team. The members
of the team were (top row,
left to right): Maxine Swift '58,
Barbara Heylman '58, Pat
Fletcher '58; (middle row, left to
right): Rosemary Deniken '57,
Betty Holton '60; (front row):
Shirley Radcliff '57 (captain).
(Arcadia University Archives)

A t-shirt worn by Beaver College students to display their protest of the Cambodian invasion during the Vietnam War. (Photo by Jerome Lukowicz, Philadelphia, Pa.; Arcadia University Archives)

By the end of the 1960s, political activities had joined the social on most campuses across America. Beaver was no exception, as students joined in protests and marches to support the Civil Rights Movement. Much in the spirit of the times, the College arranged for a weeklong exchange program with Johnson C. Smith University, an historically black institution, and ran this program for two years. Some of our students were involved in early sit-ins opposing racial segregation and took part in the first "Freedom Rides" to the South, to the extent that Beaver women are cited in histories of the period.

In the fall of 1969, students proposed a moratorium on classes to protest American actions in Vietnam and Cambodia and to express solidarity with other students (no moratorium took place on the Beaver campus). The *Beaver News*, though, coordinated campus peace actions for the colleges and universities in Montgomery County.

Long-range Planning Begins

Soon after consolidation was completed, College leaders began to consider how best to use the new, more spacious campus. They were concerned both to assess the capacity of the location, and to plan for upgraded facilities. New science facilities were needed, but would it be best to renovate Murphy Hall (the location of the sciences at the time) or to construct a new building? How many students could the 55-acre site support? In the fall of 1965, the Board decided to construct a new science building which would also contain a large auditorium which the campus then lacked. Later, in early 1967, President Gates wrote a "Look Ahead" in which he saw the Beaver of 1975, still a "college," but with 1,200 students and greatly increased participation in study abroad. Two years later, a master plan was created showing the residence halls, instructional buildings, and athletic facilities needed to meet that objective. The College took the first steps on a $45,000,000, ten-year capital campaign, in order to build that dream.

THE 1970s: CHANGE AND STRAIN

As the new decade dawned, the College found itself buffeted by economic and social changes. Repeated deficit budgets and extensive use of short-term bank financing to meet operating expenses took a toll, and banks began to call in their loans. Plans for the capital campaign fell away in the face of day-to-day pressures. At the urging of those banks, College officials sought to sell what was construed as "excess real estate," land not needed for the central educational mission. In short order, an apartment building at 777 Limekiln Pike (subsequently repurchased in 2001) and a large house on Limekiln known as The Villa were sold. The College even sought to sell or lease the 15 undeveloped, wooded acres lying west of the campus; these plans were abandoned in 1978 after two potential developers were unable to gain the needed financial backing and/or regulatory approval.

Miss Frances H. Lewis '39, Director of College Relations (1948–1980), and Vice President for Development and College Relations (1980–1981). (Arcadia University Archives)

Dr. Charles E. Moulton, Professor of Computer Science and Mathematics (1966–1992) and Chair of the Department, works with students in the original computer laboratory in the basement of Boyer Hall of Science circa 1978. He, along with Dr. Edward F. Wolff, Associate Professor of Computer Science and Mathematics (1977–) and Chair of the Departments, developed the College's computer program and facilities. (Arcadia University Archives)

Facilities Development: Plans Deferred

Of the expansive plans put forth in 1969, only one building was to result, the new science structure. The Marian Angell Boyer Hall of Science, completed in January 1971 at a cost of $3,500,000 was considered one of the finest facilities of its kind at a small college.

The other major facilities developments during the decade were modifications within existing structures. A gift of Trustee John A. Mitchell equipped ceramics and metals studios in Murphy Hall and a contribution by Trustee Mrs. Willard Hollingshead provided an additional large painting studio in Spruance Hall. The renovated second-floor chapel space (1978) in Murphy Hall was named for Frederick Stiteler whose bequest helped make it possible; the space served from its inception as a general purpose auditorium. In the summer of 1979, a computer center established in Boyer Hall enabled the College to introduce a full-scale program in Computer Science.

Enrollment Struggles and Successes

The return to coeducation was another outcome of the climate of stringency. Social change movements of the mid-1960s and early 1970s began to erode interest in single-sex education and shifted the student market in ways that adversely affected Beaver College. Once, Beaver was among the schools in the prestige rung right below the most selective "Seven Sisters." But as some of the latter became coeducational and, perhaps more importantly, as the previously all-male Ivy League schools did the same, Beaver and others like it found the pool of interested applicants shrinking rapidly. The institution saw these changes coming, and carried out a study to determine whether or not to admit men. The study recommended remaining as a women's college.

Nevertheless, and in direct contrast to the study's outcome, a critical enrollment shortfall forced the administration to decide that coeducation was essential for institutional survival. In 1973, with almost no planning or time for adjustment, Beaver College once again became coeducational (as it had been from 1876 to 1907).

The Charter was amended in 1973 to encompass the education of men, for the first time in 66 years. In addition, changes were made that severed the College's formal legal ties with the United Presbyterian Church in the U.S.A., this with the full concurrence of the Board of Christian Education. This sort of change, necessitated by the strictures on the ever-more-important Federal student financial aid, was widespread at that time, and occurred at most of the Presbyterian schools that did not have a strong religious mission. The Charter provided, however, that the College should always maintain a mutual concern with the Presbyterian Church, and Beaver (and later Arcadia) continued to be recognized as a church-related institution.

Undergraduate enrollment continued to be a challenge, however, as it was for many institutions in

Mrs. Marian Angell Boyer, member of the Board of Trustees (1962–1978), and major College benefactor. (Arcadia University Archives)

Mrs. Kathryn E. Darby '44
(1945–1987), Assistant
Professor of Biology and
Assistant Dean of Graduate
Studies, teaches a biology
laboratory in Boyer Hall
of Science circa 1971.
(Arcadia University Archives)

Marian Angell Boyer Hall of
Science, opened in 1971, was
named in honor of Mrs. Boyer,
member of the Board of
Trustees, whose generous gift
made the building possible.
(Arcadia University Archives)

American Language Academy (ALA) students welcome Beaver College students to a 1995 reception in Grey Towers. (Arcadia University Archives)

Mr. T. Edwards Townsley, Dean of Admissions (1975–1985). (Arcadia University Archives)

the early 1970s. Beaver's near total tuition dependency (relying on tuition for 80 to 90% of its revenue) made the situation acute. When Marjorie Darling retired as Dean of Admissions in 1973, the College decided that the use of an external recruiting firm could bring greater resources and wider-ranging contacts to bear upon the problem. The two-year experience with the chosen firm was a failure, as high school guidance counselors grew to resent the presence of paid professional recruiters. Now convinced that a self-run admissions effort was superior, in 1975 the College succeeded in recruiting a highly regarded admissions professional from Drexel University, Mr. T. Edwards Townsley, who served as Dean of Admissions for the next ten years.

In 1975 Beaver College entered into an agreement to rent space to the American Language Academy (ALA), a private English-language training organization with branches at a number of American colleges and universities. Beaver's was to turn into one of the longest-lived campus/ALA collaborations, bringing perhaps 6,500 international students to our campus since the program's inception. ALA typically enrolled 250 to 300 students a year, drawn from some 60 nations around the globe. Most students were polishing English skills prior to enrolling in an American college or university; not a few matriculated as Beaver students.

By decade's end, more students than ever came to the campus. With the development of new constituencies, enrollment in the fall of 1979 reached a new record high: 1,925 full- and part-time students in Glenside, and 344 students from 125 other colleges in international programs. Graduate Studies accounted for 931 students, the Evening/Weekend College for 222, and part-time undergraduates for 133. Of the 639 full-time undergraduates, the great majority were from Pennsylvania, the others were mostly from the Eastern Seaboard (a change from the more national profile of students in the fifties and sixties). Seventeen foreign countries were represented. In addition, the presence at any given time of from 60 to 75 international students at the Beaver branch of the American Language Academy lent a cosmopolitan air to the campus.

Except for the 35-year-long foray into coeducation in the late 1800s, for many years Beaver had a relatively homogeneous student body—female, white (with only an occasional nonwhite student); middle to upper middle class; by an overwhelming majority, Protestant. By 1980 the student body was characterized by diversity—in age, gender, economic level, and religion, in race and ethnic origin, in range of abilities and talents. This diversity in itself became understood as being part of the educational process. Coeducation, welcoming adult students, drawing more students from heavily Catholic local high schools, and using some especially strong links with Black Presbyterian congregations for recruitment, all contributed to this diversification.

Program Development and
a Tradition of Curricular Innovation

In the same year that coeducation began (1973), Beaver initiated its own programs leading to the Masters of Education and Master of Arts in Education, though the College had been offering courses through the Lehigh Regional Consortium for Graduate Teacher Education since 1969.[16] While these programs grew directly from the strong undergraduate Education major, the move into graduate education was another way to increase revenue. Beaver's new programs were designed to enable teachers to attend classes part-time during late afternoons and evenings and in the daytime during summers. The College anticipated a limited program with modest enrollment, but numbers skyrocketed. Certificate and master's programs in Special Education and Reading began soon after, largely in response to student demand. By late in the decade, graduate work in almost all specializations in Education were offered, including the post-master's Certificate in Advanced Studies (1979). Two additional master's programs were launched in the 1970s: an interdisciplinary program leading to the Master of Arts in Humanities (1975), one of the first of these in the nation; and, a Master of Music (also in 1975), which was withdrawn due to low enrollment four years later.

A major review of the undergraduate academic program in 1969–70 resulted in the substitution of a more conventional set of distribution requirements for the core curriculum. Some of the impetus for revision came from students who were aware of trends to reduce or eliminate required courses in colleges across the nation. Since then, students have sat on several faculty committees.

From 1973 to 1975, an ad hoc faculty committee surveyed the changing direction of undergraduates' interests across the nation. It recommended that career goals be given more prominence, that career counseling be intensified, and that a business curriculum be reinstituted.

Changes followed which realized these aims, including: a January Winterim term (1973), a month between the two semesters which could be devoted to independent research, short internships, or even mini-courses; a 3–2 plan leading to a Masters in Christian Education in conjunction with the Princeton Theological Seminary (1974), three years at Beaver, two at PTS; a two-year pre-nursing program from which students might transfer to the University of Pennsylvania (1975); Cooperative Education (1976), alternating periods of study on campus with paid employment in career-related positions; and participation in a Columbia University College of Engineering 3–2 plan (students taking their first three years at Beaver, followed by two in New York at Columbia, emerging with a B.S. in Engineering, or, with a sixth year, an M.S.). Other developments saw a substantially increasing enrollment of older adults in undergraduate

---

[16] See the accompanying essay, *A History of Graduate Studies*, pp 154–163, for more details.

Dr. William D. Biggs, Professor of Business Administration (1988–) and Chair of the Department of Business Administration and Economics, leads a small group learning activity. (Photo by Sam Nocella, Willow Grove, Pa.; Arcadia University Archives)

Mrs. Nancy Rose, first Director of the Child Care Center, 1974–1987, supervises children in the Center's playground outside Thomas and Kistler Halls in the mid-1970s. The Child Care Center evolved out of a Political Science class project of Dr. John Berrigan, Assistant Professor of Political Science (1973–1979). It was the first state licensed college-based child care center in the region and was used as a model by other area institutions. (Arcadia University Archives)

Faculty members at a Faculty Development Workshop, "Writing Across the Curriculum," led by Dr. Elaine Maimon and funded by the National Endowment for the Humanities in the mid-1970s. Dr. Maimon, Professor of English, (1973–1986), also served as Director of the Writing Program, Associate Dean for Curricular Research, and Associate Vice President for Special Projects. The picture shows faculty members (from left to right): Mrs. Helene C. Cohan (German), Dr. Gerald Belcher (History), Dr. Jo Ann Weiner (English), Dr. Elaine Maimon (English), and Dr. Barbara F. Nodine (Psychology). The person standing by the window is Dr. Linda Flower, guest workshop leader from Carnegie Mellon University. (Arcadia University Archives)

programs through intensified recruitment and the opening in 1974 of Beaver College's Child Care Center, and the reinstatement, in the same year, of undergraduate summer sessions, which had all but disappeared in previous decades.

Beaver College was shortly to attain national recognition for pioneering efforts in curriculum innovation. Through the initiative of Dr. Elaine Maimon of the English Department, Beaver secured a major three-year grant (1977–80) from the National Endowment for the Humanities to create and disseminate an innovative writing-across-the-curriculum program.

Under that program, multiple disciplines provided instruction and practice in writing throughout the students' four undergraduate years. Faculty from many departments participated in workshops to explore the teaching of composition and attended lectures by visiting experts. Ultimately, Beaver faculty became the experts, and traveled to colleges and universities nationwide to advise on the creation of writing-across-the-curriculum programs based upon our model. Several of the key faculty in this project [Drs. Maimon, Gerald Belcher (History), Gail Hearn (Biology), Finbarr O'Connor (Philosophy), and Barbara Nodine (Psychology)] joined together to publish two books about these influential developments.[17] This degree of cross-disciplinary cooperation became the norm at the College, often to the great surprise of visitors from other campuses.

In the fall of 1978, an Evening/Weekend College opened with classes in Business Administration, providing opportunities for employed adult students. Soon thereafter, it began to offer programs leading to the Associate of Arts, the Associate of Science, and the B.S. in Business Administration, and the B.A. in Computer Science.

Administrative Changes

The nearly instant early success of the graduate programs suggested that other departments might prosper by creating their own master's degrees. To oversee this effort as well as the burgeoning offerings in Education, the College created an Office of Graduate Studies and appointed Margaret LeClair its first Dean. Dr. Robert L. Swaim, chairman of the Religion Department (1954–1973), replaced Dr. LeClair as Dean of the College. Dr. Swaim served for only two years, until his retirement, and his immediate successor, Dr. John Linnell, was in office for just the 1975–76 year.

In 1977, Dr. Norman A. Miller, Chair of the Education Department since 1968, succeeded Dr. Margaret LeClair in the Graduate Dean's Office. Dr. Bette E. Landman, formerly an Assistant Professor of Anthropology, was appointed as the new Dean of the College, a title soon changed to Vice President for Academic Affairs and Dean of the College. Also in 1977, a new Dean of

Mr. Craig D. Culbert, Assistant Professor of Chemistry and Physics (1963–1993), shows students how to maintain an automobile during a 1972–73 Winterim class. (Photo by Joseph Marchetti, North Hills, Pa.; Arcadia University Archives)

[17] Maimon, E. P., Belcher, G. L., Hearn, G. W., Nodine, B. F., & O'Connor, F. W. (1984). *Readings in the arts and sciences.* Boston, MA: Little Brown and Co.
Maimon, E. P., Nodine, B. F., & O'Connor, F. W. (1989). *Thinking, reasoning and writing.* White Plains, NY: Longman, Inc.

Students, Gale DiGiorgio, came to the College. Mrs. DiGiorgio served in that capacity for the next twelve years, managing the ever-more complex world of student affairs through most of the 1980s.

As the decade drew to a close, concern began to grow, especially among the faculty, that the College was growing in unplanned ways, and that faculty needs were often being overlooked in this process. Faculty salaries (like others nationwide) had slipped far behind increases in the cost of living. A wage freeze in 1977 raised alarm about the long-term prospects for the College. Relatively stable year-to-year enrollments offered little hope for improvement. Moreover, the College had fallen into a pattern of deficit budgeting and was delinquent in repayment of the Federal building bonds it still held on the residence and dining halls and the Boyer science building. A faculty Committee on Economic Planning and Priorities began to meet with President Gates to promote greater attention to planning, fundraising and faculty welfare. This effort was to lead to several outcomes, one of which was the long-range planning begun in the 1980s.

THE 1980s: PLANNING, PROGRAM EXPANSION, AND PROMISE

The 1980s was a decade of ongoing, innovative curricular revision, new program development, and administrative change.

Continuing the Traditions of Curricular Innovation and Program Development

Based in part on the success of the faculty development/curricular change effort of the writing-across-the-curriculum project, the College received in 1981 a second, large, multi-year grant from the federal Fund for the Improvement of Post-Secondary Education (FIPSE). In this project, an interdisciplinary group met to explore issues of problem solving, critical thinking, and collaborative learning. In addition to the changes that this work brought to individual classes, the project led to the creation of Freshman Seminars. Initially, these were mandatory and focused on general orientation to college along with the three grant foci. Ultimately, Freshman Seminars evolved into a voluntary and more theme-based series of short courses in the first year. As a further outgrowth of the FIPSE grant, in 1986 the faculty modified the core curriculum once more, stipulating that courses eligible to count for distribution credit under the core must meet process goals in such areas as problem solving, critical thinking, and collaborative learning. Distribution courses were categorized into seven conceptual areas. In addition, as in the past, students were required to take at least two semesters of composition, two of laboratory science, and two semesters of physical education. By decade's end, a further change eliminated the January "Winterim" session which had by then ceased to be used by more than a very few programs.

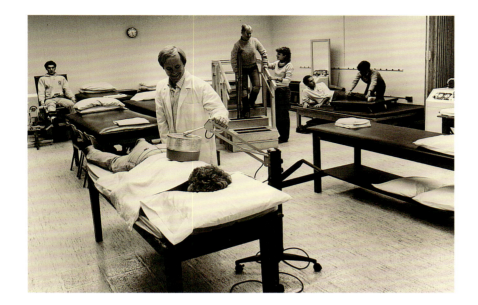

Mr. Jan S. Tecklin, Professor of Physical Therapy (1982–), and Chair of the Department (1986–1993), teaching a clinical laboratory class in the basement of Boyer Hall. The students, starting with the one on the examining table are (clockwise): Kathy McDonald Kelly, Jay Kogan, Angela Pizzo Sisler, Beth Weiss, Bruce Apple, and Marsha Berger Grant, all of the Physical Therapy Class of 1984. (Arcadia University Archives)

In 1982, Physical Therapy came to Beaver College. Dr. E. Jane Carlin '40, a Trustee and loyal alumna, was a graduate of the now-abandoned Physical Education program who had gone on to become a founder of the profession of physical therapy, along with becoming the first woman to attain the rank of brigadier general in the U.S. Army.

She proposed that the College consider starting a Physical Therapy program, at nearly the same moment as the University of Pennsylvania was discontinuing its program in this field, thus both opening a market and making faculty available (along with some equipment and books ultimately donated by Penn to Beaver's program). With great anticipation, the College accepted this idea. The advent of Physical Therapy at Beaver represented the first introduction of a new program (initially at both the bachelors and masters level; the bachelors program was phased out in a few years) that had not grown organically from existing programs, with the wholesale creation of an academic department. The existence of a master's program in a fast-growing profession became an asset for undergraduate enrollment, as the College created an "automatic" admissions channel for Beaver undergraduates who met the graduate entrance criteria. A boon to the Departments of Biology and Psychology, at its height over 40% of incoming freshmen hoped to go on to study Physical Therapy.

In contrast to Physical Therapy, the other graduate programs begun in the 1980s grew directly from existing programs. The first, a Master of Science degree in Health Education was added to the graduate offerings in Education in 1982. The English Department created a Master of Arts degree in English (1985) with concentrations in professional, creative or technical writing, writing and communications, and literary and critical studies. In the same year, the Psychology Department initiated a Master of Arts in Counseling. This and subsequent growth in graduate education was spearheaded by a new Dean of Graduate Studies, Dr. A. Richard Polis, who succeeded Dr. Norman Miller in 1980 upon the latter's retirement. Dr. Polis remained as Dean for the next twenty years.

In 1982 the College added educational programming for students at the upper end of the age scale. A group of local retired citizens, many of whom had audited courses on campus for the prior six years, determined to organize their own program for educational and cultural enrichment. Thus, the Community Scholars was born, with administrative support from the College. Hundreds of senior citizens each year have participated in short courses and trips to musical, theatrical, and artistic events, bringing added diversity and good will to the College.

Unplanned Administrative Changes

Administrative change at the start of the decade had momentous effects on the future of the institution. In the early summer of 1982, President Gates became ill

Dr. E. Jane Carlin '40, member of the Board of Trustees (1960–1997). (Arcadia University Archives)

127

Dr. Bruce Wilson,
President (1983–1985).
(Arcadia University Archives)

Dr. Bette Landman,
President (1985–).
(Arcadia University Archives)

Dr. Ellington M. Beavers,
member of the Board of
Trustees (1980–), and Chair
(1984–1989). (Photo by
Robert C. Scanlon, Paoli, Pa.;
Arcadia University Archives)

with what was ultimately a terminal illness. Dr. Bette Landman, at the time the Vice President for Academic Affairs, stepped in as Acting President for the uncertain period of President Gates's absence. Dr. Landman quickly began to reengage the faculty in a planning process, responding to the pent-up sense of frustration about this matter among faculty and others. A set of initial institution-wide goals was established, and detailed plans were created to achieve them.

Progress in implementing these plans was interrupted, however, when, in January 1983, President Gates died and a formal presidential search ensued. Though an internal candidate existed, there was a strong sentiment that only an outsider could give the College the energy it needed to move forward. Dr. Bruce Wilson, formerly the Vice President for Academic Affairs at Elizabethtown College, was appointed in 1983.

The two years of his presidency did not lead to the kind of progress that had been hoped for, and his resignation in 1985 left the College again in a precarious leadership position. After an extended hunt in consultation with an executive search firm, the Board determined that the need could best be met by choosing among strong internal candidates, and, in 1985, selected Dr. Bette Landman to be the College's first female President. Mr. Lloyd Abernethy, a professor of history and one of the senior-most members of the faculty, consented to step into the Dean's role vacated by

Dr. Landman until a permanent successor could be found. In August of 1986, Dr. Jean Dowdall was appointed to succeed Dr. Landman as Vice President for Academic Affairs and Dean of the College. Dr. David Gray, Vice President and Director of the Center for Education Abroad (CEA), resigned during this period, and his position was taken by Dr. David Larsen. Throughout these years of rapid change, the College benefited from the strong leadership of Board Chair Dr. Ellington Beavers.

Formal Strategic Planning Begins Again, and Has Results

President Landman soon began to reactivate the dormant planning process, and over the next several years the College planned and took the major initiatives which together crafted the university that emerged at the turn of the century. The planning discussions identified several areas of deficiency that were believed to be impeding institutional progress. Among these were: lack of a clearly defined mission and focus, chronic financial instability and over-reliance on tuition and CEA surpluses, a persistent gender imbalance (male undergraduates had never been more than 15 to 20% of the population), non-competitive faculty and staff salaries, and aging campus facilities that had not kept up with the rapid advances in technology.

As a first step in collecting the data upon which to base planning decisions, the College applied for and received a grant to underwrite an extensive market research

study of present and prospective students, attempting to learn what attracted and did not attract students. The results clearly showed that the then current athletic facilities (i.e., the gymnasium area in Murphy Hall and a steeply sloping playing field) were a deterrent to both male and female students, and that the College name, long known to have been a source of embarrassment to some young people due to its slang connotation, was also a difficult barrier for potential applicants to overcome.

A newly established College Planning Council then began to craft a new mission statement for the institution, hoping that such a document would serve as a touchstone for future planning. That statement, reproduced below, articulated for the first time the international component of the mission, a feature that would come into sharper focus in the following decade.

> Beaver College prepares students for life in a rapidly changing global society. As a comprehensive, independent institution, Beaver offers men and women a broad range of undergraduate and graduate programs on its suburban Philadelphia campus and through its Center for Education Abroad.
>
> Beaver College prides itself on meeting the changing educational, career, and developmental needs of students, alumni, and the local community while emphasizing the strengths of a liberal education.
>
> Non-sectarian, with strong ties to the Presbyterian Church, Beaver College is committed to serving students of all

ages and cultural backgrounds. A dedicated community of teacher/scholars, administrators, staff, trustees and students work in genuine collegiality to create a climate for learning and personal growth based upon intellectual challenge and nurturing relationships.

At Beaver College, the following qualities define educational excellence:
• Skill in critical thinking and effective communication
• Mastery of a major field of knowledge
• Appreciation of multiple disciplinary perspectives and methods of understanding
• Proficiency in applying what is learned
• Ability to work productively in culturally heterogeneous groups
• Understanding of the integral relationships among the peoples of the world
• Commitment to ethical decision making and socially responsible community participation

Since its adoption in 1987, through the change to Arcadia University, and up until the date of this publication, this statement remained at the forefront of institutional planning and assessment.

The College then took advantage of its 1989 self-study, part of the regular Middle States Association reaccreditation process, to reengage in formal planning. Concrete results soon emerged. Many facilities needs faced the College, but the planning process led to the strategic decision to build an athletic building. Thus, in 1993 the College dedicated its first new building in over two decades, the Kuch Athletic and Recreation Center,

Kuch Athletic and Recreation Center opened in 1993, containing athletic and fitness facilities, classrooms, and the bookstore. This picture shows the front of the building viewed from the parking lot. (Photo by Larry Salese, Philadelphia, Pa.; Arcadia University Archives)

A men's basketball game in the Alumni Gymnasium in the Kuch Athletic and Recreation Center. (Photo by Larry Salese, Philadelphia, Pa.; Arcadia University Archives)

The Lenox Pool, in the Kuch Athletic and Recreation Center, was named in memory of J. Stanley and Dorothy L. Lenox, parents of Jean Lenox West '57, whose generous gift made the pool possible. (Photo by Larry Salese, Philadelphia, Pa.; Arcadia University Archives)

named for long-time Trustee and donor Harry Kuch and his wife, Catherine. One of the finest structures of its kind when it opened, Kuch contained regulation basketball courts, 1,500-seat bleachers, training, dance, weight and exercise rooms, the Lenox Pool (a gift of alumna Jean Lenox West '57) plus two classrooms and the bookstore.

To fund this construction, as well as to increase the endowment and strengthen annual giving, the College forthrightly undertook its first capital campaign since the catastrophic effort of the 1920s and several unsuccessful attempts to launch campaigns in the 1970s and 1980s. The $10,000,000 target included $5,000,000 for the Kuch Center, $3,000,000 in enhanced annual giving, and $2,000,000 for endowment. The five-year "Foundation for the Future" Campaign was co-chaired by Board Chair Lowell "Tim" Thomas and alumna and Trustee Marilyn Cranin '54, while Trustee Harry Kuch and alumna Jean Lenox West served as Honorary Co-chairs. The Board as a whole played an important leadership role in the fundraising. At its conclusion in 1995, $12,100,000 had been raised, more than 20% above the goal.

Credit for the first successful capital campaign was due to many hundreds of donors, and to the spirited work of the newly reorganized Office of Institutional Advancement. Vice President for Advancement Jay Vogel had been hired in 1986 with the mandate to reinvigorate fundraising. About 20% of the alumni contributed annually, a level that had not changed for many years. Mr. Vogel and his staff created a series of donor recognition clubs, a significant expansion of communication with and activities for alumni, new activities to educate students about alumni responsibilities, and, ultimately, the Alumni Walk of Pride (a walkway with paving blocks bearing the names of alumni donors). These steps would lead to annual alumni contribution rates climbing above 40% by the end of the century, a level at the top 10% of all colleges and universities in the United States. Other achievements included securing the first two named faculty chairs in the modern history of the institution—The Stacy Anne Vitetta '82 Professorship (a gift of Mr. and Mrs. Francis G. Vitetta in memory of their daughter) and the Frank and Evelyn Steinbrucker '42 Professorship (a bequest from Frank Steinbrucker and Evelyn Kordes Steinbrucker)— and the beginning of a program of planned giving intended to bolster the endowment. Through careful cultivation of donors, and a growth-oriented investment and spending policy, that endowment grew from $269,000 in 1980 to $30,000,000 by 2000.

THE 1990s AND BEYOND: MOSTLY MOMENTUM

A Crisis Starts the Decade

The tale of the 1990s was, overall, one of sustained growth, innovation, and expansion, but it was not without setbacks. The most important came in 1991, just

131

Andrew Johnson '02 works in the Fine Arts Department's digital imaging studio in the renovated gymnasium area of Murphy Hall in the late 1990s. (Photo by Stacy Kelly, Arcadia University, Glenside, Pa.; Arcadia University Archives)

Mr. Hugh G. Moulton, member of the Board of Trustees (1991–), and Chair (1998–2002). (Photo by Jon D. Adams, Hi5 Photos, Jenkintown, Pa.; Arcadia University Archives)

as enthusiasm for planning was growing. The national economic downturn in the early nineties resulted in an unexpected drop in demand for on-campus housing, threatening the delicately balanced budget of the College operation in Glenside. At the same time, the sudden onset of the Persian Gulf War caused unprecedented cancellations in CEA enrollment, resulting in a substantial operating loss (though the CEA and the College operating budgets had been separated for several years). For the first time in memory, the College was forced to make layoffs in order to balance the Glenside operating budget—about 15% of the administrative and support staff. Employee morale, consequently, suffered a setback. These events stimulated a long-range planning process in CEA, targeting program expansion and growth, and a further restructuring of the CEA/College financial relationship. The Chair of the Trustee International Programs Committee (and later Board Chair), Mr. Hugh Moulton, was instrumental in moving that planning process forward.

From the start of her tenure, President Landman had worked to sever the prior financial dependence on annual CEA surpluses, and rather, as the Board mandated, sought to balance the College budget without CEA contributions. CEA would henceforth also seek to balance its operational budget, and was permitted to capture half of its surplus as a quasi endowment to guard against unpredictable reversals in the future, with the remaining half of the surplus directed to the College endowment.

A Spirit of Growth Resumes

A quick succession of new buildings and programs helped to revive spirits. A newly articulated strategic plan, with ambitious five-year enrollment goals, found its targets surpassed in only three years. A planned expansion in the size of the graduate Physical Therapy class was used to underwrite the construction of a new, two-story instructional building. When finished in 1994, the classroom portion of the new Health Sciences Center, named for alumna Dr. E. Jane Carlin, was linked to the round Ruck building which was renovated to serve as faculty offices (health services were moved to the ground floor of Heinz Hall).

Construction equipment had only just left the campus when plans were made to build a new residence hall, expand the Dining Hall, and renovate portions of Murphy Hall. All three projects were completed by 1997, responding to rapid growth in enrollment, and in keeping with the long-range plan. The residence hall, named Knight Hall after the College mascot, featured the first suite-style housing on campus; the expanded Dining Hall doubled the eating space and created social and performance spaces on the ground floor. The changes in Murphy Hall eliminated the old gymnasium and replaced it with new art, computer design, and communications studios and music offices. These projects, and the new Carlin Wing of the Health Science Center, were funded by bond sales backed by the prospect of tuition from expanded enrollment. This, the first new debt financing

The Health Sciences Center
was built in 1994 to house
the expanded Physical
Therapy Department.
It incorporated the Ruck
Health Center, which was
remodeled to form faculty
offices. The Health (Wellness)
Center was moved to the
ground level of Heinz Hall
in the space formerly
occupied by the Post Office.
(Arcadia University Archives)

Knight Hall, opened in 1997, with suite-style rooms. In addition
to student housing, Knight Hall houses the offices of Student
Affairs, Career Services and Cooperative Education, and the
Department of Modern Languages. (Photo by David DeBalko,
Huntingdon Valley, Pa.; Arcadia University Archives)

133

at the College in over thirty years, represented a shift in attitude among the Trustees, more sophisticated financial management in the Treasurer's Office, and a growing confidence in the fortunes of the College. For the first time, Beaver bonds qualified for financial ratings.

Program Development and Innovation

On the undergraduate level, grant-funded faculty development projects led to further curricular innovation. With major support from the Knight Foundation, the College first explored the introduction of service learning components in several majors. To set the tone, a day of service was incorporated into Freshman Orientation, resulting in about 1,000 person-hours of community service each year.

Next came intensive, inter-institutional collaboration to seek new models of liberal learning, spearheaded by Associate Dean Susan Gotsch-Thompson and professors Jo Ann Weiner (English), Robert Thompson (Political Science) and Dennis Kuronen (Fine Arts). This resulted in the creation of a new General Education Program in 1994, this time with a true core of common experience. Two inter-disciplinary, team-taught courses were required of all new students: Justice: Multicultural Interpretations, and Pluralism in the United States. A further outgrowth of the Knight funding (as well as of the grant-funded curricular developments of the prior decade) was the requirement that all majors have senior capstone programs resulting in formal, public presentations of the students' final projects.

The General Education Program retained the composition and laboratory science requirements of the prior program, as well as reformulated distribution requirements, and added new requirements in foreign language and mathematics achievement.

As this General Education Program was being implemented, senior administrators and a growing number of faculty had come to recognize that a strong commitment to internationalization was both an educationally sound and achievable goal to pursue. The presence of CEA, now sending abroad nearly 2,000 students from other U.S. colleges and universities annually, seemed like an underutilized resource. Scarcely any Beaver students studied abroad—about three to six a year. How could the campus culture be changed to make international experience and understanding a desired outcome? The answer took many forms. Most obvious, in 1994, was the creation of the London Preview Experience, a program which took about 70% of the freshman class to London for a week during spring break, for a nominal fee—$150 for the first several years. The result of a "wild" idea by education faculty member Dr. Jeffrey Shultz in a brainstorming planning session, this program became a significant mark of distinction by decade's end. In addition, CEA resources were used to send substantial

numbers of faculty overseas to meet with colleagues in our partner institutions. Ultimately, between these journeys and participation in London Preview (faculty and staff accompanied the freshmen) nearly all full-time faculty (and most of the staff as well) had some sort of recent overseas experience. As well, faculty were consistently encouraged to counsel students about the advantages of study abroad, and overseas courses were listed in the College catalog. In less than five years, Beaver went from sending six students abroad through CEA to sending nearly 100 (not counting the London Preview). Other study abroad opportunities were created in the form of courses with a week or two of foreign travel embedded within them. By 2002 fully one-third of the graduating seniors had some kind of credit-bearing international experience, and national organizations began to recognize the College as a leader in international education.

A new major was introduced in 2002, a Bachelor of Fine Arts in Theater. Developed by Assistant Professor David Bassuk, the emergence of this degree coincided with a revival of extensive theater programming at the institution.

The story was not just one of program growth. Taking seriously its obligations to review the quality of existing programs, the faculty moved to discontinue three programs over this period. After 1996, the College no longer offered its two associate's degrees (A.A. and A.S.) These were never a major source of students and were felt to be inconsistent with the level of education to which

the institution aspired. The formal Weekend College was also disbanded.

New graduate programs continued to be developed, both derived from existing programs and created anew. Of the latter sort were a Master of Science in Genetic Counseling (1994) and a Master of Science in Physician Assistant Studies (1995) that became a Master of Medical Science in 2002. Combined with Physical Therapy, these new programs helped to establish a strong, full-time graduate population in the health sciences. Genetic Counseling, at its inception one of very few such programs in the nation, was a response to suggestions by the local health professionals. Physician Assistant Studies, the eleventh such program in the nation, was created in part to provide a countervailing program to the Physical Therapy program as competition from other institutions in the latter field began to challenge enrollments. A Master of Health Administration program, begun in 1994, combined courses offered in Health Education and Business Administration; due to low enrollment, this program was suspended in 2001. In 1998, two new developments at the graduate level served as harbingers of things to come. The first, a highly innovative Master of Arts in International Peace and Conflict Resolution, had the unique feature of a second year of study and internships wholly overseas. The second was the conversion of the Physical Therapy program to a three-year, entry-level doctoral degree (D.P.T.). This

The cast of a modern version of Shakespeare's "As You Like It" presented in 2001 at the Little Theater under the direction of Mr. David Bassuk, Assistant Professor of Theater Arts (1991–). (Photo by David Bassuk, Arcadia University, Glenside, Pa.; Arcadia University Archives)

A computer lab in the former Browsing Room of Atwood Library. (Photo by Ed Wheeler, Radnor, Pa.; Arcadia University Archives)

was consistent with the trends in the discipline, but it caused the College to wrestle with the issues of whether to offer doctoral level education.

Academic Recognition

As the College sought ways to elevate both the aspirations of students and the reputation of the institution, academic administrators and faculty began to investigate membership in nationally recognized honor societies. In 1994, Beaver College inaugurated its chapter of Phi Kappa Phi, a national honor society recognizing undergraduate achievement (this replaced Lambda Delta Alpha, a strictly local honorary society). Alpha Epsilon Lambda, offering similar honors to graduate students, was inaugurated in the same year.

Other, program-based honor societies have been regularly added since the 1950s: Pi Delta Phi (French), 1958; Phi Alpha Theta (History), 1964; Sigma Zeta (Computer Science and Mathematics), 1979; Phi Delta Kappa (Graduate Education), 1980; Sigma Delta Pi (Spanish), 1991; Sigma Beta Delta (Business Administration), 1996; Pi Sigma Alpha (Political Science), 1998; Alpha Sigma Lambda (Continuing Education [adult] students), 1999; Chi Alpha Epsilon (Act 101 and Gateway students, those in special programs for economically and educationally disadvantaged students), 2000; Sigma Tau Delta (English), 2001; Phi Beta Delta (international study and scholarship), 2002.

Faculty and staff too have been honored for their outstanding achievements. Beaver College has participated in the Lindback Foundation program of recognizing excellence in teaching since 1961, and since 1987 we have taken part in the Council for the Advancement and Support of Education's annual Professor of the Year awards. Internal awards are also given in the forms of a research fellowship donated by Trustee and former Board Chair Dr. Ellington Beavers, annual awards for faculty service, and a staff award named for Martha Washington, a long-time and impeccably reliable housekeeping worker.

Technological Change

The revolution in personal computing which started in the 1990s put most small colleges at a disadvantage. The needs for infrastructural overhaul and never-ending equipment renewal were well beyond the budgets of all but the best endowed institutions. Beaver College met some of this challenge by joining in a consortium of eight local private colleges. Dubbed the Southeastern Pennsylvania Consortium for Higher Education (SEPCHE), the consortium has been able to raise and share $14,000,000 over eight years from Federal and private sources. Initially, these funds were devoted at Beaver to the electronic automation of library catalogs, then, to creating high-speed data networks throughout the campus, and ultimately, to faculty development in the areas of enhancing learning aided by electronic technology. SEPCHE also sponsored

A faculty show, featuring satirical skits, has appeared sporadically over the decades. This 1981 show featured a cast (from left to right) of Dr. Finbarr W. O'Connor (Philosophy), Dr. Samuel M. Cameron (Psychology), Mrs. Gail DiGiorgio (Dean of Students), Dr. Mark P. Curchack (Anthropology), Dr. Frank Schwartz (Political Science), Dr. Peggy Maki (English), Mr. Tony Giampietro (Audio-Visual Services), the patient (reputed to be Dr. William Barker, Education), Dr. Jo Ann Weiner, partially visible (English), and Althris Shirdan (Sociology) enacting a skit from the television soap opera *General Hospital*. (Photo by Harlan Udis '91, Huntingdon Valley, Pa.; Arcadia University Archives)

faculty and staff training workshops and took advantage of economies of scale in certain joint purchases.

Student Life at the End of the Century

Undergraduate life at the end of the 20th century was characterized by a cycle of dances, concerts, and films, along with a set of campus-specific festivities and a significant degree of community service. Among the highlights were a Masquerade Ball at Halloween, the "Snowball" semi-formal dance in December, and the spring-time Cotillion semi-formal, all sponsored by the student-run Residence Hall Council. "Spring Fling" had become a regular feature in the calendar, consisting of a carnival-like "Blitz" event, an outdoor band festival called "Woodstock," and a lip-sync contest. The most idiosyncratic event, however, was the "Mr. Beaver Contest," a male, Miss America-style "beauty" pageant, in which entire residence floors or commuter groups sponsored and supported contestants. On occasion, the faculty would put on their own satirical show.

Community service activities, beyond the service learning components of several classes, succeeded in involving large sectors of the student body in work designed to help the less fortunate residents of the region. Organized service work took place on Martin Luther King Day, and, as noted above, a day of service had become a feature of New Student Orientation. Orientation itself was a form of service, as over 60 undergraduates each year organized and ran the entire orientation program. Service organizations came to campus regularly to recruit students, and the Student Government mandated that all student clubs devote a portion of their fee-generated funds to service activities.

The opening of Kuch Center served as a catalyst for expansion of our athletic profile, as the College joined the prestigious NCAA (Division III). Beaver had been an early member of the PAIAW—Pennsylvania Association of Intercollegiate Athletics for Women—in the halcyon days of the early 1970s. While this fostered league competition, it did not allow for post-season championship play, and so in the 1980s the College joined the NAIA (National Association for Intercollegiate Athletics). In 1992, Beaver became a charter member of the Pennsylvania Athletic Conference, a group of similar-sized institutions with like resources and philosophy for athletics.

The advent of male students in the early 1970s changed the athletic landscape at the College, though at first numbers were too small to allow for a robust set of male teams. However, by the mid-1990s, men's teams (in such sports as soccer, basketball, tennis, and baseball) began to have some success, as did some of the women's teams. With more specialized coaching, better equipment and training, and (after the 2000 addition of regulation softball, hockey and tennis facilities), the ability to practice at home, more success followed in the form of league championships and occasionally trips to regional NCAA finals.

Michael Jeffers '01, second baseman, completes a double play. (Photo by Brian Ferreira, Haddon Heights, N.J.; Arcadia University Archives)

Students relax and have fun during Spring Fling. (Photo by Brian Ferreira, Haddon Heights, N.J.; Arcadia University Archives)

Heather Sherwood '01, women's softball player, connects with the ball. (Photo by Jon D. Adams, Hi5 Photos, Jenkintown, Pa.; Arcadia University Archives)

A group of students pose after work on a Habitat for Humanity project on Martin Luther King Day, 2000. (Arcadia University Archives)

During the 1990s, and beyond, the institution continued to benefit from outstanding leadership in the many realms of student life in the person of Dr. Janet Walbert, Vice President for Student Affairs and Dean of Students. She worked to see that sufficient student personnel staff were in place to meet the challenges of a more crowded campus with accelerating demands for student support.

Administrative Changes

Several changes in administrative ranks took place in the middle of the decade. In the summer of 1993, Vice President for Academic Affairs Jean Dowdall left to assume the presidency of Simmons College. Her place was taken by Dr. Michael L. Berger, formerly the Head of the Division of Human Development at St. Mary's College of Maryland. From 1986 to 1992, the ever-more competitive task of student recruitment had been under the guidance of Mr. Neil Holtzman, Dean of Admissions. When he left the College in 1992, Mr. Dennis Nostrand was recruited to the newly created position of Vice President for Enrollment Management. By effective use of electronic technology to manage the recruitment process, unifying recruitment and financial aid, and employing innovative (and frequently award winning) marketing techniques, Mr. Nostrand produced a steady rise in both the numbers and entering SAT scores of the undergraduate population, to the levels detailed below.

MOVING TOWARD THE SESQUICENTENNIAL: A NEW NAME FOR A UNIVERSITY-TO-BE.

The trends of the 1990s—new programs, new buildings, and growing enrollment—spilled over into the new millennium. Planned program expansion, this time of the Physician Assistant Program, led to the construction of a new instructional building. Brubaker Hall, opened in 2000, named by alumna Sara Brubaker Steer in honor of her mother, was the College's first fully wired, "smart" classroom building, able to employ the latest in instructional technologies. It was also linked by a bridge to the Carlin Wing of the Health Sciences Center, establishing synergy between graduate-level health programs. New graduate programs continued to be developed: a Master of Science in Public Health (2001) and a second doctoral program, a Doctor of Education in Special Education (2002).

Rapid program and enrollment growth led to a critical parking shortage. This was solved by creating new spaces on the site of the former hockey field and tennis courts, while reestablishing those athletic fields, plus a regulation softball field and athletic pavilion, on the wooded hill adjoining the main campus. The tennis courts were named for Betty Holton Weiss '60, a champion tennis player while a student and on the senior circuit, Women's Basketball Coach from 1966 to 1970, and Tennis Coach from 1975 to 1995; the new hockey/softball fields were named for Rosemary Deniken Blankley '57, an outstanding athlete at Beaver and long-time Chair of the Annual Fund.

Using additional proceeds available from the construction bonds for Brubaker Hall, the College began a program of purchasing houses on streets contiguous to the campus to use both as places to house offices and to serve as a land bank for potential further expansion. An apartment complex across from the campus at the corner of Church Road and Limekiln Pike, once owned by the College, was repurchased in 2000 to accommodate the growing resident population.

In the same year, CEA purchased an office structure at 1601 Church Road to house a mushrooming staff that had outgrown its space on the second floor of the Castle, thus establishing an eastern outpost of the campus. The Castle rooms returned to student residence space.

The quality of student housing underwent many changes during the 1990s and into the new century. The institution learned to refer to the buildings in which students lived as residence halls, reflecting the fact that they were more than places to sleep, but rather the "homes" of the students. The opening of Knight Hall and the purchase of the apartment complex at 777 Limekiln Pike expanded greatly the variety of housing stock. Record enrollments achieved in 2002–03 forced the University to rent space for students in other nearby apartment complexes. Housing policy changed as well, when, after several years of discussion and debate, the Board approved the possibility of mixed-gender housing in special circumstances, in stark contrast to the parietal rules of only 30 years before.

Status and Name Change

As the year 2000 approached, the College found itself in an unusual situation. The successful plans of the past decade had brought enrollment beyond the levels first imagined in 1967. Full-time undergraduates surpassed the 1,200 goal (reaching 1,266), and part-time under-graduates numbered 362. Graduate students numbered 1,109 (195 full-time and 914 part-time). This growth of students was matched by increases in the faculty. Long-stable at about 65 full-time faculty, by century's end the number stood at nearly 90, along with 10 to 15 adjunct professors with full-time teaching loads, plus about 200 part-time faculty providing instruction, many in the part-time and professional programs. Budgets had been balanced for almost a decade. The endowment had grown more than tenfold and alumni donations were strong. A reputation for academic excellence, and for international education, had solidified. Planners decided to confront the leading strategic steps which had yet to be addressed: whether to become a university, and whether to change the institution's name.

The question of becoming a university was relatively easy to answer. The institution had, for a number of years, been a university in fact, thanks to the size of its graduate program. Market research revealed that being called a university might be an asset to recruitment, and would almost surely help in corporate fundraising and in overseas relationships. While formally becoming

A time-lapse photograph of
the PECO building in downtown
Philadelphia announcing
"Beaver College Is Now
Arcadia University" as part of
the name change celebration.
(Photo by Edward Savaria, Jr.,
newcommunications.com,
Philadelphia, Pa.; Arcadia
University Archives)

Students, alumni, faculty,
staff, and friends celebrated
the announcement of the
institution's new name,
Arcadia University, at a
surprise midnight event on
November 20, 2000. A signing
banner enabled everyone to
leave his or her mark on the
historic evening. The students
pictured signing the banner
are (from left to right): Melissa
Romano '03, Jen Bach '01,
Tiffany Miller '02, Heather
Cowdrick '01, Mandy Schorle
'01, and Rose O'Brien '01.
(Photo by Jon D. Adams,
Hi5 Photos, Jenkintown, Pa.;
Arcadia University Archives)

University President Bette E. Landman (left) symbolically presents the first Arcadia diploma to Linda Vandegrift Gazzillo '90, President of Arcadia University's Alumni Association. (Photo by Jon D. Adams, Hi5 Photos, Jenkintown, Pa.; Arcadia University Archives)

Students representing the three major divisions of Arcadia University are pictured with their respective administrators: (from left to right), Jeff Tingle '02, undergraduate who has taken part in international studies through Arcadia's Center for Education Abroad; Dr. David Larsen, Vice President and Director of the Center for Education Abroad; Dr. Norah Peters-Davis, Dean of Undergraduate Studies and Faculty Development; Corinne Royer '02, President of the Student Government Organization; University President Bette E. Landman; Dr. Mark Curchack, Dean of Graduate and Professional Studies; Ingrid Chung '02M; and Dr. Michael L. Berger, Vice President for Academic Affairs and Provost. (Photo by Jon D. Adams, Hi5 Photos, Jenkintown, Pa.; Arcadia University Archives)

The new Landman Library opened during the 2002–03 academic year. The 26,000 square feet added to the existing structure effectively doubled the size of the library. (Photo by Mark Curchack, Arcadia University, Glenside, Pa.; Arcadia University Archives)

a university took an application to the State to accomplish, it was a change that was never in doubt.

Adopting a new name was, of course, of far greater moment. It had been clear for years that the negative connotations of the word "beaver" had depressed undergraduate inquiries and acceptances to the point that the College had to work about three times harder to recruit a class than did comparable institutions. At the same time, the name was both a source of pride and embarrassment to alumni of different vintages and outlooks. In the spirit of collegiality and openness which had been hallmarks of the institution for decades, the College began a process of inquiry and deliberation regarding the name, first by way of a large opinion survey of alumni, friends, students, faculty and staff. Encouraged by the results to pursue a change, a faculty/staff/alumni/trustee/student committee met through the summer of 2000 to identify a potential new name for the institution, one that would capture its present and hoped-for future essence. Several potential names were tested in nationwide focus groups and reviewed by attorneys for trademark and related issues. The most popular name, and one which passed the legal and focus group tests, was suggested by Dr. Joan H. Thompson, Associate Professor of Political Science. In October of 2000, the Trustees approved, and on November 20, 2001, it was publicly announced, that Beaver College would become Arcadia University. The official change of name and status took place at a formal ceremony on July 16, 2001.

The attainment of university status provided the necessary stimulus for a formal reorganization of the Academic Affairs unit of the institution. Dr. Michael L. Berger, who had served ably as Vice President for Academic Affairs since 1993, was given the additional title of Provost. Reporting to him were two newly appointed Deans: Dr. Norah Peters-Davis, who had been an Associate Professor of Sociology, and then Associate Dean, became the Dean of Undergraduate Studies and Faculty Development; Dr. Mark P. Curchack, formerly the Executive Assistant to the President and Assistant Professor of Anthropology, became the Dean of Graduate and Professional Studies. Dr. A. Richard Polis, Dean of Graduate Studies since 1980, had retired in 2000.

Finally, as this volume is published, the University opens a new library, doubled in size and remodeled throughout to meet the needs of 21st-century education. The original campus library, built for an undergraduate school of 600 students, had long since become too small and out of date. The new structure forms a counterbalance at the north end of campus to the dominant Grey Towers Castle on the south, and was funded by a second capital campaign in less than a decade, this one of $11,000,000. In the fall of 2001, it was decided to name this expanded and renovated structure the Landman Library, in honor of the much beloved and respected President whose tenure had seen so many positive changes.

Dr. Norah D. Peters-Davis, Associate Professor of Sociology (1991–), Chair of the Department of Sociology and Anthropology (1994–2000), and, since 2001, Dean of Undergraduate Studies and Faculty Development. (Photo by Jon D. Adams, Hi5 Photos, Jenkintown, Pa.; Arcadia University Archives)

GREY TOWERS CASTLE: HISTORIC LANDMARK, CONTEMPORARY TREASURE

AN ESSAY

Michael L. Berger[1]

INTRODUCTION

Grey Towers Castle has been a symbol of Beaver College and Arcadia University for generations of students, faculty, staff, and administrators, especially those who have attended or worked on the Glenside campus since 1962.

From its promontory on the southwest corner of the campus, the Castle looks down upon a modern and growing campus of over 55 acres and is, itself, the object of spectacular views from the second floor of the Landman Library.

The historical background of the Castle and its architectural elements has been well documented by Professor Emeritus Kenneth Matthews[2]. The life of the man who commissioned Grey Towers Castle, William Welsh Harrison, is the subject of a study by Marie T. Gallagher[3], Administrative Assistant to a succession of academic deans and vice presidents here. The purpose of this essay is not to duplicate that information, but rather to place it in the context of the multiple uses to which the Castle has been applied by Beaver/Arcadia. The most important of the 41 Castle rooms will be discussed in terms of their original function and the subsequent one(s) they performed for the College and University from 1929 to 2003. As will become increasingly obvious, Grey Towers Castle has been an exemplar of the adaptability of an architectural landmark to changing uses for three-quarters of a century.

As is explained in more detail elsewhere in this book, in 1925 Beaver College moved from Beaver County, Pennsylvania, to Jenkintown. The College thrived there and by 1929, with a student enrollment of 600, a need for expansion led the College to purchase the former country estate of William Welsh Harrison in Glenside. The focal point of the newly acquired property was Grey Towers Castle, which at the time of its construction in the late 19th century was purported to be the third-largest private residence in the United States.

[1] Thanks to President Bette Landman, Dr. Norman Johnston, Dr. David Larsen, Marie Gallegher '95, Lois Roemmele '58, and Kay Darby '44 for sharing their knowledge of the Castle. Descriptions of the interior design of the Castle draw heavily upon the work of Professor Emeritus Kenneth D. Matthews, to whom I am grateful.
[2] Kenneth D. Matthews, (n.d.). *The story of Grey Towers: A great American castle*. Glenside, Pa.: Arcadia University; Kenneth D. Matthews, (1985). *Grey Towers Castle: A living landmark*. Glenside, Pa..: Beaver College.
[3] Marie T. Gallagher, (1995). *In search of William Welsh Harrison and his legacy*. Unpublished bachelor's thesis, Beaver College, Glenside, Pa.

Harrison was one of four brothers who inherited the Franklin Sugar Refining Company from their father, and thereby became a very wealthy man. In 1881, William and his wife of one year, Bertha White, and their baby daughter Geraldine moved to a 47-acre estate in Cheltenham Township called Rosedale Hall. Working with a young, unknown architect, Horace Trumbauer, Harrision built a stable (Murphy Hall) on the estate property. Harrison planned to upgrade and renovate Rosedale Hall itself, but, in January of 1893, the mansion caught fire and burned to the ground.

Undaunted, he turned once again to Horace Trumbauer, the beginning of whose illustrious career can be traced to the commissions that Mr. Harrison gave him for Grey Towers and other buildings on the estate. At Harrison's request, Trumbauer designed the exterior of his home to resemble a medieval English castle. Grey Towers is built primarily of Chestnut Hill gray stone—hence the name—and Indiana limestone was used for trimming the doors and windows and for the gargoyles and grotesques leering out from the towers and parapets. The Castle was commissioned in 1893 and completed about 1898. It was declared a National Historical Landmark in October 1985.

We may never know just why Harrison desired such an impressive structure. It seems almost certain that he intended to entertain his peers on a grand scale, but there is no evidence that such a social life ever developed. Perhaps key to this was Harrison's early estrangement from his wife, and his flagrant romance with a wealthy widow named Isabella Fishblatt. When William Harrison died in 1927, his will left large sums to Fishblatt, to whom the entire estate would devolve if Bertha Harrison and surviving son William were to die without issue. Under those circumstances, Beaver College's 1929 offer of $712,500 for the Castle, all the estate buildings, and 138 acres, was hard for Mrs. Harrison to refuse.

FIRST FLOOR

As one enters the Castle through the massive main doors on the east side, the atrium of the Great Hall reception area remains essentially the same as Trumbauer intended it to be. Designed to impress, even awe, visitors to Grey Towers, it has succeeded in doing that since 1898.

Rising three stories to a coffered, barrel-vaulted ceiling and reflecting the French Renaissance style of Chambord, it features two impressive fireplace mantels of Caen marble,

The Great Hall and Grand Stairway as they appeared at the middle of the 20th century. (Arcadia University Archives)

145

the mahogany Grand Stairway and balustrade leading to the Music Room landing, wainscoting, and a solid mahogany floor. (As impressive as the stonework is on the fireplace mantels, the fireplaces are merely decorative—not intended to be functional and thus lacking flues.)

At various times, the Great Hall has been viewed as a "lobby" area, where visitors are asked to wait prior to business appointments or social dates, and has usually been furnished accordingly. On occasion, it has served as the venue for special events. For instance, it is a regular site for concerts, weddings, and other celebratory affairs, with the Grand Stairway often forming the backdrop or the platform for formal pictures. The staircase itself has even served as the focus of co-curricular activities; e.g., functioning as the "stage" for the May Day Queen and her court and for a modern dance performance.

On a landing at the top of the Grand Stairway, between the first and second floor, is the Music Room, another one of those areas that has changed little in terms of design from Trumbauer's original plans. It still features windows made of leaded Belgian glass, a beautiful Baumgarten wool and silk tapestry from 1898 showing an allegory of music, and carvings of musical instruments in the woodwork. At the opposite (north) end from the tapestry is a fireplace and intricate mahogany mantelpiece. The College used the room for musical performances (at least through the mid-fifties); at one time it had an electric organ, and it still boasts a working piano.

Nonetheless, the room has always served primarily as a lounge for students residing in the Castle. Prior to the 1960s, when parietal hours regulated who could enter/exit Grey Towers and at what time, the Music Room served as an excellent vantage point from which to observe the comings and goings of one's roommates and male visitors in the Great Hall without being too obvious. (The bolder students leaned over the balcony banisters for the same purpose.)

The Harrisons had intended to engage in extensive entertaining, and the two main rooms on the north (right) side of the Great Hall certainly reflect that. The elegant Ballroom in the northwest corner, now known as the Mirror Room, is done in a Louis XV or Baroque style. It was the only major room of the Castle completely renovated by the Harrisons. The walls and ceiling were created in France and shipped to Glenside in 1900, along with the workmen to install it. Of particular note is the magnificent François Lafon ceiling painting of the four seasons, along with the mirrored doors (after which the room gets its contemporary name), and the gold vine motif ornamentation. In addition to being a venue for formal and informal dances, along with the adjoining Rose Room, the Mirror Room has functioned as a perfect locale for chamber concerts, musical recitals, poetry readings, lectures, receptions, special presentations, and even meetings of the Faculty and of the Board of Trustees.

The Rose Room, so named by the College because the cupids in the center ceiling painting are holding roses, and garlands of those flowers are the principle element in the two other paintings that flank it, also features bronze chandeliers, and cream and gold silk

The Grand Stairway being used as a stage for a modern dance performance, probably in the late 1940s or early 1950s. (Photo by Harry J. Utzy, Jenkintown, Pa.; Arcadia University Archives)

Students performing in the Music Room on the landing at the top of the Grand Stairway. (Photo by Harry J. Utzy, Jenkintown, Pa.; Arcadia University Archives)

The Drawing (Rose) Room as it was furnished in the 1920s when the Harrisons still resided in the Castle. (Arcadia University Archives)

Students relaxing in the Rose Room in the late 1960s or early 1970s. The settee in the right foreground was left behind when Mrs. Harrison sold the Castle to Beaver College in 1929. (Photo by Harry J. Utzy, Jenkintown, Pa.; Arcadia University Archives)

Students dancing the twist in the Mirror Room in the early 1960s. (Photo by Joseph Marchetti, North Hills, Pa.; Arcadia University Archives)

brocade wall fabric (replaced by flocked wallpaper in 1969). Originally designed to be the Drawing Room, it is the only area that we know the Harrisons used for social gatherings. It served the College for a number of years as a student lounge, albeit an oversized one.

Students down to the present will recall a settee along the wall between the windows on the east side, one of the few pieces of furniture that Mrs. Harrison left behind when she sold the estate to the College. One of the first television sets owned by the College was located in this room in the 1950s, as well as a cabinet housing a "hi-fi" to play the vinyl records of the era. Together with the Mirror Room, it has often and continues to serve as the venue for celebratory, catered lunches and dinners.

The Mirror and Rose Rooms were restored in 1969 through a generous gift of Marion Angell Boyer (Mrs. Francis Boyer). At that time, the floors were sanded, the walls painted, and wall sconces and other metal work were re-gilded. The floors remained the original ones until the summer of 1996 when the one in the Mirror Room had to be replaced because it could no longer be refinished due to excessive wear and repeated sanding. In 2001, water damage and structural stress created a situation where the ceiling in the MIrror Room and its beautiful Lafon painting were in imminent danger of collapse. The room was closed for seven months while the ceiling was repaired. The University took advantage of this situation to re-gild and enhance the wattage of the wall sconces and to install air conditioning in this room and the Rose Room, thus expanding the number of months that these facilities could be used comfortably.

Unlike the north side, the functions of the rooms to the south of the Great Hall have changed considerably since the Harrison period. The alcove immediately to the left as one enters the Castle has a lengthy history of service as the location for the College/University telephone operator, although the old, hand-operated switchboard and its multitude of cables has given way to an electronic system. Staffed now primarily by University Public Safety personnel, in the past it was a prime source of employment for students in need of financial assistance.

Beyond the phone operator's station are rooms designed by the Harrisons to be a wood-paneled library. Since the consolidation of the Jenkintown and Grey Towers campuses, it has served as the presidential office suite. Next to it, as one moves toward the rear of the building, is the space the Harrisons used as their formal Dining Room. It features an impressive chandelier, two fireplaces, walls containing carvings of forks, knives, and plates in the Ionic walnut wood panels, and a deeply decorated plaster ceiling. It was lavishly furnished, with a solid mahogany table running the length of the Dining Room with matching chairs. The pantry in the middle of the north wall served that function and doubled as the location of the family safe. Despite the intent to host formal dinners in this room for Philadelphia's high society, the Harrisons actually did little entertaining here, and one can imagine Mr. and Mrs. Harrison seated at opposite ends of the huge dining table, their physical distance from each other a reflection of their personal relationship.

With the College's purchase of Grey Towers in 1929, this area continued to serve as a dining room, but one that now provided meals (and banquets) for the students residing on the Glenside campus. While the function remained the same, the change in the ambiance of this room was striking as can be seen in the accompanying photographs.

Beginning in 1962, with the completion of the new dining hall and residence hall complex and the consolidation of all operations on the Glenside campus, this space ceased to be a dining area. By the mid-sixties, it had become home to the Development, Public Relations, and Alumnae Offices, and subsequently functioned as the first office of the Center for Education Abroad. It is unlikely that uninformed visitors in 2003 would guess its original use, as free-standing room dividers have been used to create cubicles that serve as the workstations for members of the Enrollment Management staff.

Next to the old Dining Room is an area that the Harrisons called the Breakfast Room. Approximately half the size of the former, it still featured wood paneled walls and a stone fireplace. A large glass and metal extension, featuring a domed roof, was added onto the south side of the Breakfast Room in 1907. It was intended to be a sunroom, and the original exterior wall and windows were removed to facilitate movement between the two areas. It was to this space in the Castle that the "Chatterbox," later shortened to "Chat," a place where students could go for light refreshment and conversation with their classmates, was successfully transplanted from the Jenkintown campus. This was one of the few places on campus where students were allowed to smoke in the 1950s. When the new residence halls and dining hall were built on the east side of the campus in the 1960s, the Chat was relocated there. Since then, the two interconnected areas have served a multiple number of service functions, but are now in the process of being renovated for some grander use.

The space west of the Breakfast Room, which had served the Harrisons as a kitchen, pantry, dining area for the servants, and an adjoining "hall," is the area of the Castle that has undergone the most significant changes in terms of architecture and function. Walls have been constructed to create a suite of offices that have served since 1962 as a location for Admissions/Enrollment Management activities.

Returning to the Great Hall, the naïve visitor would be hard-pressed to find the Billiard Room, hidden as it is behind the Grand Stairway, on a sunken landing a half-level below the Great Hall floor. Victorian society was a gendered one, with clearly demarcated roles and spaces for men and women. One key manifestation of that aspect of society in Grey Towers Castle was the design and placement of the Billiard Room. With its oak paneled walls, iron lighting fixtures, a painted leather frieze above the paneling, and playing cards represented on the fireplace, it was a male preserve.

A women's college of the 1930s had no need for such a room, and it was soon converted to other uses. Best remembered, perhaps, are the years when it functioned as the apartment for the Castle Housemother and, later, the Director of Residence. (A bronze plaque

The Dining Room as it appeared in the 1920s when the Harrisons still ate there. (Arcadia University Archives)

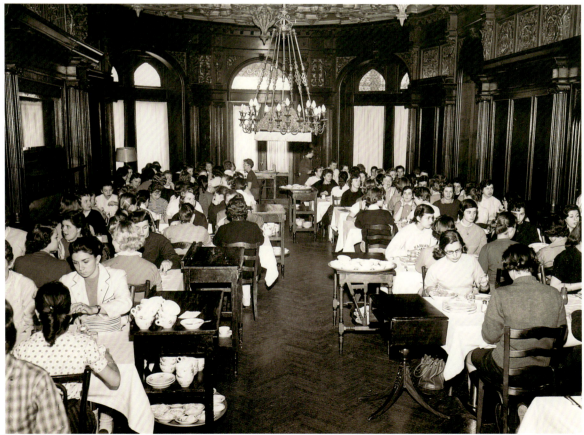

Beaver College students eating in the Dining Room, probably in the late 1950s or early 1960s. (Photo by Harry J. Utzy, Jenkintown, Pa.; Arcadia University Archives)

engraved with the latter designation remains on one of the sliding pocket doors to this day.) This single room was furnished and configured in such a way that it served as a bedroom for the housemother/residence director, provided a living room where she could entertain students and guests, and even contained a small kitchenette for preparing meals. It was later transformed into a conference room, where meetings are held and occasionally classes are taught.

SECOND FLOOR

The marriage between William Welsh Harrison and Bertha White was not a particularly happy one. Trumbauer's design for the second floor bedrooms clearly foresaw William and Bertha spending their nights alone. As Marie T. Gallagher has observed in her study of Harrison and his legacy: "His wife, Bertha lived in one half of the Castle and he in the other. . . . Even the drastically different decor of his apartments compared to those of his wife would indicate separateness about them. They were like ships passing in the night, existing at opposite ends of a vessel, sailing down an immense mahogany stairway, only to meet at meals across an expansive table of empty talk." (1995, p. 38)

If these architecturally interesting and well-appointed second floor apartments were the locations of little happiness within the Harrison family, the same cannot be said of generations of students who have lived in them (and the third floor rooms) during their undergraduate years. Unlike most college residence halls, the Castle has offered an unusual and appealing lifestyle, one that has been eagerly sought since the 1930s to the present. Comfortably housing 70 or more students when there were no administrative offices on the second floor, the spacious rooms are ample evidence of the lavish style in which Mr. and Mrs. Harrison and their children lived. Beds, bureaus, and chairs for up to eight students in each suite are intermingled in what essentially are large living rooms, and those with adjoining alcoves have additional flexibility in terms of how furniture is arranged in the space.

With the building of new residence halls in the early 1960s as part of the consolidation process, fewer students had to be housed in the Castle, and certain areas on the second floor ceased to be student rooms. For instance, in the mid-sixties a portion of Mr. Harrison's apartment became a guest bedroom for campus visitors. Later, the offices of the Center for Education Abroad (CEA) were moved into the suite that defined Mr. Harrison's side of the Castle. That space remained the Center's main office in the United States until 2000, when all functions of that unit were moved to 1601 Church Road. The area of the Castle that had been occupied by CEA was then returned to its original collegiate function as residential rooms for women undergraduate students.

Across the atrium, Mrs. Harrison's apartments also were transformed into office space in the 1960s. Her former bedroom has served for some time as additional space for the Admissions (Enrollment Management) Office. The adjoining area that functioned as Mrs. Harrison's dressing room was initially used as supplementary office space for CEA,

Mrs. Harrison's bedroom on the second floor of the Castle, as furnished in the 1920s. (Arcadia University Archives)

Students relaxing and studying in their Castle residence, probably in the late 1950s or early 1960s, in the space that was formerly Mrs. Harrison's bedroom. (Photo by Harry J. Utzy, Jenkintown, Pa.; Arcadia University Archives)

later served primarily as the home to the Office of Human Resources, and since 1997 has functioned as space for the growing Enrollment Management staff.

THIRD FLOOR

Comparatively little is known of how the Harrisons used the third floor of the Castle. A common misconception is that that was where the servants in the household lived. Actually, they were housed in a separate structure built diagonally across from the power plant on the west side of the property. In reality, the rooms on the top floor were occupied by the two Harrison children, William Welsh, Jr. and Geraldine, and by occasional guests.

Geraldine's suite, located in the corner, consisted of a bedroom and adjoining bath, together with a private living room. Despite the fact that she died a century ago, Geraldine has played a continuing role in Castle lore. In 1902, she eloped with a flamboyant older man named John (Jack) Anderson. After a few months living at Grey Towers Castle, the newly married couple set up housekeeping at 2121 Walnut Street in Philadelphia, with furniture and treasures borrowed from the Castle. Their happiness, however, was to be brief, for in less than a month Geraldine became ill and quickly died. Geraldine was buried from her childhood home, Grey Towers, where she had lain in state.

Generations later, when Beaver College students began to occupy the upper floors of the Castle as a residence hall, stories began to circulate of an apparition that was occasionally seen walking the halls—a ghost believed to be that of Geraldine, going to and from what had been her third floor bedroom, reliving the happy childhood days of her brief life in the only home that she had truly known. These legends were buttressed by the misbelief that Geraldine had hanged herself in the Castle (usually, this was said to have happened in Mr. Harrison's blood-red smoking turret on the second floor). Students reported sightings of the Castle ghost throughout the latter half of the 20th century.

A CONCLUDING COMMENT

Grey Towers Castle has become an icon that symbolizes Beaver College and Arcadia University. Partially, that status stems from the Castle's historical importance and the physical prominence of the building itself. Equally significant has been its permanence and adaptability, traits that also have served Beaver and Arcadia well as that institution has evolved into a comprehensive university of national renown.

A group of students enjoying a pizza in one of the large residence rooms in Grey Towers Castle in 2000. (Photo by Ed Wheeler, Radnor, Pa.; Arcadia University Archives)

A HISTORY OF GRADUATE STUDIES AT BEAVER COLLEGE AND ARCADIA UNIVERSITY

AN ESSAY

A. Richard Polis[1]

Dr. A. Richard Polis, Professor of Education (1968–2000), Chair of the Department (1977–1982) and Dean of Graduate Studies (1980–2000). (Photo by Larry Selese, Philadelphia, Pa.; Arcadia University Archives)

Graduate education at Arcadia University began in 1969, when the presidents of several liberal arts colleges, working with Dr. John Stoops, the Dean of Education at Lehigh University, formed the Lehigh Regional Consortium. The Consortium was designed to expand the reach of Lehigh's Graduate School of Education and allow it to focus on doctoral students. Member colleges in the Consortium would offer a small number of Lehigh University master's level education courses on their respective campuses. Income would be shared between the institutions, and faculty at the host institution would be allowed to teach some of the courses. The Lehigh Regional Consortium for Graduate Teacher Education started its operation in the summer of 1969.

Since the courses would be offered in early afternoon or evening, with little or no cost to the institution, Beaver agreed to join in this endeavor and earn some much-needed income. Allentown College of St. Francis deSales (now DeSales University), Marywood College, Ursinus College, Wilkes College, Moravian College, and Lehigh University were the other original members of the consortium. Dr. Norman Miller, Chair of the Education Department, represented Beaver College at the initial meetings.

It did not take very long for enrollment to grow and for students to be drawn to the possibility of taking graduate level courses in Glenside. By the summer of 1972, 83 had enrolled in five courses, or an average of 16 students per course. Clearly, a number of local teachers wanted to study at Beaver College and a number of faculty in education, English, chemistry, psychology, and other disciplines wanted to teach them. Soon, students started to inquire about the possibility that Beaver might start its own graduate degree programs. At that time few small colleges in our geographical area, other than Bryn Mawr, offered graduate programs. It was of concern that competition would come from large institutions such as Temple University, the University of Pennsylvania, and Lehigh University. Some faculty thought the idea was

[1] Thanks to the following individuals (listed in alphabetical order) for contributing their remembrances and for checking facts: Dr. Fred Baus, Chief Executive Officer of the Colleges of Worcester Consortium; Professors Samuel Cameron, Andrea Crivelli-Kovach, Michael Dryer, Rebecca Craik, Deborah Eunpu, William Frabizio, Steven Gulkus, Warren Haffar, Jeffrey Shultz, Joan Thompson, and Richard Wertime, all of Arcadia University; and Harold Stewart, Registrar of Beaver College and Arcadia University for over thirty years.

impractical, others felt it was pretentious. How could Beaver College, with its already understaffed and over-worked faculty of 60 men and women, begin to offer even one graduate degree?

To answer that and other questions, the College engaged Dr. Stoops as a consultant to evaluate the idea of graduate studies at Beaver and to report his findings to faculty and administration. Dr. Stoops recommended that Beaver start a graduate program in education and indicated in his report that a program of approximately 100 students a year could be expected once it were established. Based on the recommendations of the consultant, the advocacy of the Education faculty, and the strong demand from local teachers, the Board of Trustees in late spring of 1973 authorized the establishment of master's degree programs to begin with the summer session 1973, and Dr. Margaret F. LeClair was appointed Dean of Graduate Studies. Within a year, 300 students had been admitted to those programs, and the first Beaver College master's degrees (7 in number) were conferred in May 1974.

In a related initiative, Dr. A. Richard Polis of the Education Department was appointed Director of Off-Campus Services in 1974. In this capacity, he opened several off-campus sites at which graduate education courses were offered. The idea was to expand Beaver's geographical bounds by offering classes north near Doylestown, west at Cabrini College, east near Newtown, and south in the School District of Philadelphia. Students who took courses at these sites were required to do at least 15 credits of graduate study on the Beaver campus if they wished to complete the master's degree. Enrollments in these off-campus courses reached several hundred every year and brought students from as far as the state of Delaware.

Dr. Norman Miller, Professor of Education (1967–1977), Chair of the Department, and Dean of Graduate Studies (1977–1980). (Arcadia University Archives)

A third venue for graduate education courses resulted from our affiliation with the Schuylkill Valley Nature Center (SVNC). Mrs. Kay Darby, Assistant to the Dean of Graduate Studies, in concert with Mr. Richard James, SVNC Coordinator, created and nurtured an environmental education program. This program became a concentration within the Master of Arts in Education degree and was one of only two such programs in Pennsylvania. The fact that Beaver had affiliated with SVNC gave the program credibility in the community of environmentalists and environmental educators.

The number of graduate students continued to grow at an unexpected rate in the subsequent years, doubling annually for several years until reaching a population of more than 800 in master's level Education programs alone. In 1977, Dr. LeClair retired, and Dr. Norman A. Miller was appointed to succeed her as Dean of Graduate Studies. In just a few short years, graduate enrollments reached the size of programs in the once-feared neighboring universities. For a tuition-dependent institution like Beaver, this was good news indeed.

Such growth was a testament to the quality of the faculty, to able administrative leadership, and to the dedication of the Graduate Studies Office staff. In 1980, Dr. Norman Miller resigned his post as Dean of Graduate Studies because of poor health. Dr. Polis was appointed Dean, but still retained his position as Chair of the Education Department while the Education programs underwent the periodic accreditation review by the Pennsylvania Department of

Education. Upon the successful completion of that task, Dr. Polis resigned the departmental chairmanship in 1982, and Dr. Ronald Rowe was asked to take the helm. Dr. Rowe tightened and consolidated the programs that had been developed under Drs. Miller and Polis. He remained in the chair until 1985, at which time Dr. Jeffrey Shultz was lured away from the University of Cincinnati to head the department. With extensive background in university teaching and research, Dr. Shultz was to head the Education Department for the next twelve years, a period that witnessed considerable growth both in programs and student enrollment.

With the incredible success of the master's degree programs in education, faculty and administration began to discuss whether it might be possible to expand graduate programming into areas other than teacher education. An entrepreneurial spirit was emerging that would lead to multiple programs in new fields, with a total enrollment that by the end of the century would rival that of the undergraduate student population.

One of the first programs to emerge from such discussions was one in the burgeoning area of health education. An affiliation with Lankenau Hospital was forged in the mid-seventies and led to a concentration in health education within the M.A. in Education degree, developed and coordinated by Ms. Kay Darby and Ms. Barbara Quigley, Health Education Coordinator for Lankenau Hospital. By 1982, this concentration in health education had grown, as had the interest in that field from health professionals, nurses, health and physical education teachers. The response from the College was development of a full-fledged Master of Science in Health Education degree, implemented in the mid-eighties.

Given its interdisciplinary nature, it was not immediately apparent how the new Health Education degree fit within the College's administrative structure, and for the next decade it searched for a logical "home." At first, it was housed in the Biology Department, then oversight passed to the Graduate Studies Office, and finally it was placed under the purview of the Education Department. In 1994, Dr. Anne Hewitt was hired as a faculty member with responsibility for directing the Health Education degree. She soon realized that a complementary degree program in Health Administration, one that utilized courses in management and business administration, would benefit both the original Health Education program and the College as a whole. Dr. Hewitt approached Dr. William Biggs, Chair of the Business Administration and Economics Department, with her idea. Dr. Biggs enthusiastically embraced it, leading eventually to a new master's degree in Health Administration and the incorporation of both that degree and the older Health Education one under the umbrella of the newly renamed Department of Business/Health Administration and Economics.

The emergence of graduate programs in Education and Health Education, and their subsequent success and evolution, showed that the College was quite capable of launching degrees in professional fields. Whether or not it would be equally able to successfully develop graduate programs in the liberal arts remained to be seen. In the fall of 1975, the Office of Graduate Studies charged a committee of three faculty members with the task of drawing up plans for a master's level humanities program. The resulting proposal encountered some opposition from the Graduate Dean, Dr. Margaret LeClair, who disliked its utilization of undergraduate courses. Nonetheless, it had the support of the new Dean of the College, Dr. John Linnell, and the faculty in the humanities disciplines, and that alliance proved sufficient to spearhead approval in 1975 of a new Master of Arts in Humanities (M.A.H.) degree. The underlying reason for adding this degree was the limited number of undergraduate offerings and lagging student interest in the humanities. It was suggested that by offering upper-level undergraduate courses in the humanities and recruiting graduate students to take these classes along with undergraduate juniors and seniors that the enrollment in the humanities would begin to increase.

Early in its history, the program attracted mostly teachers interested in expanding their knowledge of the humanities. The success of the M.A.H. did little to expand the undergraduate offerings, but it did increase graduate offerings in the humanities. As the program grew under the leadership of four program coordinators, Dr. Gerald Belcher (History), Dr. Finbarr O'Connor (Philosophy), Mr. Lloyd Abernethy (History), and Dr. Richard Wertime (English), it expanded its view of the humanities, adding disciplines and recruiting students from varied fields both in and outside of the traditional humanities departments. As a result, graduates of the program began to include computer scientists, attorneys, physicians, businessmen and women, as well as K–12 teachers.

With the phenomenal growth of the graduate education programs at the College and the development of the M.A.H. degree, interest and pressure developed to add additional graduate degrees in the liberal arts. Dr. William Frabizio, Chairman of the Music Department, was experiencing a great deal of success in drawing students to his music courses, which were part of the graduate degrees in education and the humanities. He was convinced that a large number of local musicians and music teachers would be excited about a Master of Music degree. A proposal was quickly developed and approved, and the new degree was instituted in 1975–76, the same year that the M.A.H. degree was introduced. In the beginning, there was much enthusiasm for the music degree, enrollments were good, and more faculty members were hired. Unfortunately, its success was short-lived, a reflection of cuts in art and music education in the public schools. In 1979, the Master of Music Degree Program was withdrawn due to low enrollment.

The College had learned a valuable lesson: not all new graduate programs were destined to succeed. Nonetheless, on balance, the College's entry into graduate education in the 1970s had been a positive development, bringing greater financial stability and curricular opportunities than would otherwise have been possible. Additional expansion seemed inevitable as the new decade began.

Thus, during the 1980–81 academic year, Dr. E. Jane Carlin, a member of the Board of Trustees and one of the pioneers in the field of Physical Therapy, suggested that the College start a Master of Science degree in Physical Therapy. This would be the first full-time graduate program in the College and there was concern about bringing such a degree forward. An outside consultant from the University of Pittsburgh was hired to make a recommendation regarding such an initiative. The consultant suggested that Beaver offer both an entry-level master's program and a bachelor's degree in Physical Therapy. At this time, the University of Pennsylvania had decided to phase out its School of Allied Medical Professions. This opened up the market and meant that personnel and material from the Penn Physical Therapy Program might be available to launch such a program at Beaver. The confluence of these developments led to a decision to move forward. Mr. George Logue was hired in 1981 to write the curricular proposal, develop the program, chair the department, and hire the faculty. His proposal, designed to accommodate as many as 20 undergraduates and 40 graduate students, gained the necessary approvals in 1982. The first graduate class recruited 30 students, and this number increased yearly.

Mr. Michael J. Coveney,
Controller (1989–2000),
Vice President for Finance
and Treasurer (2000–).
(Photo by Jon D. Adams,
Hi5 Photos, Jenkintown, Pa.;
Arcadia University Archives)

The Physical Therapy (PT) Program continued to grow and prosper and yet the space allocated to the department did not keep pace with its size and quality. Given this situation, Mr. Jan Tecklin, the Department Chair, proposed that a new facility be built to house the program. Working with Controller (later Vice President for Finance and Treasurer) Michael Coveney, he developed a proposal that would finance the cost of this new building through the additional revenue that would be generated by increasing the size of the PT cohort from 50 to 70 students per year. The increase in tuition monies also would underwrite the cost of the new faculty members needed to teach the additional students. This idea of funding construction through program expansion proved to be convincing to the rest of the faculty, the senior-level administration, and the Board. Plans for a Health Sciences Center were developed and the building, incorporating the old Ruck Health Center, was dedicated in October of 1994. (A similar scenario was followed in the late 1990s to construct Brubaker Hall, primarily to house an expanded Physician Assistants Program.)

At approximately the same time that George Logue was developing the initial PT Program, Dr. Richard Polis, who had succeeded Dr. Norman Miller as Dean of Graduate Studies, suggested to Dr. Sam Cameron that a master's degree in Counseling Psychology would be good for the Psychology Department, for practicing teachers in the geographic area, and for the College. Dr. Cameron seemed to be very interested in pursuing the idea, and such a program was approved during the 1984–85 academic year. In the fall of 1985, 16 students matriculated into the program and approximately ten degrees have been conferred yearly since then. In 1989, a School Counseling track was added to the program.

While he was facilitating the development of the Counseling Psychology Program, Dean Polis also suggested to the Department of English that it consider initiating a graduate program in English. Since the English Department had been offering graduate courses as part of the M.A. in Education degree and had been heavily involved in the teaching of graduate courses in the Lehigh Regional Consortium as early as 1969 (see above), it seemed natural that they should consider offering a Master of Arts in English. Dean Polis also believed that with the large concentration of secondary schools within a ten-mile radius of Glenside there would be many people interested in a degree in English rather than in education. A proposal for this new degree was brought forward and approved in 1985. Professors Janice Haney-Peritz, Pradyumna S. Chauhan, and Richard A. Wertime have directed the Master of English Program since then.

As the 1980s came to a close, what were to become the three pillars of graduate education at Beaver College/Arcadia University—master's degree programs in education, the health sciences, and the liberal arts—were firmly in place and approximately 47% of the students at the College were enrolled in graduate programs. The next decade was to witness a further expansion of programming in each of those areas, including the introduction of the College's first doctoral program.

In 1991, Donna Goodwin, a member of the Philadelphia Genetic Counseling Group, wrote a letter to Dr. Sam Cameron in which she noted that there were no Genetic Counseling programs in the Philadelphia area and suggested that Beaver College would be a good place to start such a program. Dr. Cameron referred her to Dean Polis who, in turn, invited several faculty from Biology, Health Education, Psychology, Physical Therapy, and Sociology to discuss the possibility of starting such a program. From that group, Dr. Raymond Rose, Professor of Biology, emerged as the point person and it was he who took responsibility for developing a draft proposal.

In the summer of 1992, a meeting was held at Beaver College to which interested faculty and local genetic counselors were invited to discuss the proposed program and the needed resources. By the spring of 1993 a proposal for a Master of Science in Genetic Counseling was completed, a process that may have been unique in terms of the support and participation of local professionals in the field. The Faculty and the Board of Trustees subsequently approved the proposal. Deborah Eunpu, a prominent Philadelphia area genetic counselor and editor of the *Journal of Genetic Counseling,* was hired as program director, and spent the 1994–95 academic year developing the specifics of the curriculum and recruiting the first class. Nine students matriculated in the fall of 1995 in what was the College's second full-time graduate health science program. By the year 2002, 58 students had graduated from the program and accreditation had been secured from the American Board of Genetic Counselors.

While the proposal for a genetic counseling program was working its way through the approval process, a college-wide planning meeting held in the spring of 1993 identified a projected upsurge in the demand for individuals trained as physician assistants and considered the logic of adding such a program to our health science offerings. During the 1993–94 academic year, Dean Polis drafted a proposal for such a degree and then reviewed that proposal with various campus advisory groups. In 1994 he organized an external advisory committee that consisted of physicians, public health specialists, academics, and faculty from

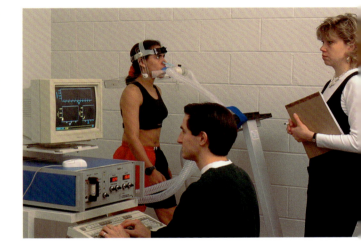

Physical Therapy students (from left to right) Christopher Lippo '97M and Sarah Wenger '97M do research in the exercise physiology laboratory with Dr. Kathleen Kline-Mangione, Associate Professor of Physical Therapy (1995–). (Photo by Anthony B. Wood, Ardmore, Pa.; Arcadia University Archives)

Beaver and engaged a consultant from the University of Iowa. Completing the developmental process took most of the fall of 1994 and a few months in the spring. A final draft of the proposal was presented to and approved by the faculty and the Board of Trustees in the spring of 1995.

The first Chair of the Department of Physician Assistant Studies was Dr. Evan Angelakos, M.D., Ph.D., former Dean of the School of Medicine at Hahnemann University. Dr. Angelakos was hired to recruit the faculty, to admit the first class of students, and to see that the Council on Accreditation of Allied Health Education Programs gave the program preliminary accreditation. Dr. Angelakos accomplished these tasks over a 15-month period and then resigned as Chair to once again become a medical school dean. Mr. Michael Dryer replaced him, with experience as a hospital administrator and a physician assistant making him well suited to oversee the implementation of the program, the further development of the curriculum, and establishment of sites for clinical rotations. Under Michael Dryer's leadership, the program secured full accreditation, and grew in size and quality, securing recognition as one of the top twenty such programs in the United States.

As these new health science programs were being introduced, attention was also given to expanding master's level offerings in the liberal arts. It was suggested by many that the extensive overseas contacts of the Center for Education Abroad might serve as the source for one or more graduate programs with an emphasis on internationalization. Some of our undergraduate students had taken courses in peace studies abroad at centers in Ireland and Austria and were enthusiastic about the experience. Dr. Joan Thompson, Co-Chair of the Political Science Department, was particularly interested in offering a master's degree program in International Peace and Conflict Resolution and started to write a proposal with advice from Dean Polis. The program that emerged was a two-year one, requiring that all second year students take graduate courses and complete internships abroad. This was unique in a field where other programs admit international students, but do little to encourage their U.S. students to study or intern abroad. In 1998, an M.A. in International Peace and Conflict Resolution (IPCR) received formal approval, and its new director, Dr. Colette Mazzucelli, began recruiting the first class for the fall semester of 1999. The first six graduates received their degrees at Commencement in May of 2001.

Dr. Mazzucelli, however, had resigned in the spring of 2000 to seek a more research-oriented position elsewhere. Dr. Warren Haffar, who had joined the IPCR faculty earlier that year, replaced her. The class recruited for the 2000–2001 academic year was again small, and the College administration began to question whether the program was financially viable. Fortunately, faculty members and academic administrators familiar with the program and its potential were able to convince the decision-makers to continue it. Many people were loath to eliminate a program that seemed so in keeping with the College's mission of preparing students for life in an increasingly global society. An extensive recruitment campaign was launched and changes were made to the curriculum to improve its attractiveness to potential students.

As a result, the program increased cohort enrollments to the point that they are almost three times the size of the original group, offerings were expanded, and the year abroad was strengthened as a learning experience. The IPCR program established affiliations with graduate programs in seven countries on three continents, along with corresponding internship sites.

In the late 1990s, new program initiatives and administrative changes occurred in the health sciences. Dr. Hewitt left the College and her position as head of the Health Administration and Health Education Programs, and Dr. Andrea Crivelli Kovach was hired to replace her. Under the latter's leadership, a new program leading to the degree of Master of Science in Public Health (M.S.P.H.) was designed during the 1999–2000 school year and was approved that spring by the faculty and Board of Trustees. The existence of an M.S.P.H. Program made the master's degree in health administration somewhat redundant. That, in combination with low enrollments in the latter program, led to a decision to suspend it following the implementation of the M.S.P.H. The graduate programs in health education and public health remained in the Department of Business/Health Administration and Economics until 2001, when the Physician Assistant Studies Department invited Dr. Kovach to move them into the renamed and expanded Department of Medical Science and Community Health. The complementary nature of the programs she oversaw and the one for preparing Physician Assistants was obvious, with the potential for symbiotic relationships. Thus, Dr. Kovach accepted the offer with the concurrence of the full faculty.

Meanwhile, the program in Physical Therapy was increasingly receiving national attention and recognition, ranked among the top ten programs in the country by one prominent newsmagazine. By the mid-nineties, Dr. Rebecca Craik, who succeeded Jan Tecklin as chair of the department, had become convinced that the future of Physical Therapy education lay in doctoral studies. She oversaw a feasibility study to investigate whether the Master of Science degree could be phased out and replaced with the Doctor of Physical Therapy (D.P.T) degree. The study determined that this was a logical move, one calculated to keep the Beaver program in the forefront of PT training in the United States. A proposal was developed and the necessary approvals secured during the 1997–98 academic year. The thorny issue of whether the College, with its limited personnel and library resources, should have any doctoral programs was resolved by determining to limit such programs to ones that were of an applied, as opposed to research, nature. Thus, a D.P.T. was feasible, whereas a Ph.D. was not. Students enrolled in the master's degree program at the time the D.P.T. was approved were given the option of completing their studies on the master's level or transferring into the doctoral program. The doctoral program began in the fall of 1998. The final group of master's degree recipients graduated in May of 2000, and the first class of doctoral students was "hooded" on May 16, 2002.

During the same time period, a significant era in the leadership of graduate studies came to an end with the retirement of Dean A. Richard Polis in June of 2000. When Dr. Polis

President Bette E. Landman presents Dr. A. Richard Polis, Dean of Graduate Studies, a plaque commemorating the establishment of a scholarship in his name at the May 2000 Commencement. (Photo by Jon D. Adams, Hi5 Photos, Jenkintown, Pa.; Arcadia University Archives)

Dr. Rebecca Craik, Professor of Physical Therapy (1983–) and Chair of the Department (1993–), adjusts the hood of Betsy Castor during the Hooding Ceremony held for the first class of Physical Therapy doctoral students the evening before the May 2002 Commencement. (Photo by Jon Adams, Hi5 Photos, Jenkintown, Pa.; Arcadia University Archives)

162

was promoted to the deanship in 1980, he realized that graduate studies could only succeed if they became an integral part of academic life throughout the College, and that meant that programs had to be created in areas other than education. Thus, he stimulated the development of master's degrees in fields such as English, psychology, and the health sciences. In addition, he suggested that it was time to expand the education program to include a doctorate in educational leadership. Throughout his tenure as dean, Dr. Polis encouraged faculty to expand their horizons and to consider new and different ways of offering graduate degree and certification programs. As a result, ten new graduate degree programs were added during his twenty-year period (1980–2000) as Dean.

The search for a new Dean of Graduate Studies began shortly after Dr. Polis announced his retirement. Maureen Guim, long-time Assistant Dean of Graduate Studies, served with distinction as Interim Dean during the 2000–01 academic year as a national search was conducted for Dr. Polis' successor. In the end, it was determined that the best candidate was already in the University's employ. Dr. Mark P. Curchack, former faculty member in the Department of Sociology and Anthropology and Executive Assistant to President Bette Landman since 1987, was selected as the Dean of Graduate and Professional Studies and assumed his new responsibilities in the summer of 2001. The expanded title was indicative of the University's enhanced interest in offering programs tailored to the needs of working professionals in the community.

Dr. Mark P. Curchack, Assistant Professor of Anthropology (1977–1986), Executive Assistant to the President (1987–2001), and Dean of Graduate and Professional Studies (2001–). (Photo by Dave DeBalko, Huntingdon Valley, Pa.; Arcadia University Archives)

With the implementation of the D.P.T., interest was rekindled within the Department of Education and the University at large for the creation of one or more doctoral (Ed.D.) degrees in education. Over the years, the success of the department's master's degree programs had led to periodic discussions regarding the advisability of introducing the doctorate in education. The Education Department had considered several possible Ed.D. programs from as early as 1986. In 1997, Dr. Phyllis Newcomer succeeded Dr. Jeffrey Shultz as departmental chair, and two years later Dr. Steven Gulkus assumed that position. Under Dr. Gulkus's leadership, the Department further explored possible Ed.D. programs. An Ed.D. in Special Education (spearheaded by Dr. Christina Ager), was brought to and approved by both the Faculty and the Board in the spring of 2002, and the first cohort of degree-seeking doctoral students in education began their studies in the fall of 2002.

The approval of the first doctoral degrees, together with the institution's change in status from college to university in July of 2001, represented a true watershed in the history of Beaver/Arcadia. Beginning as a satellite enterprise of another institution, graduate education at Arcadia University had grown to the point where nearly half the students on the Glenside campus were enrolled in one of twelve distinctive advanced degrees in the College of Graduate and Professional Studies. Further growth seems inevitable, as Arcadia faculty members explore new opportunities to provide additional master's and doctoral degrees to meet the needs of professional practitioners.

THE CENTER FOR EDUCATION ABROAD:
A LEADING FORCE IN INTERNATIONAL STUDY

AN ESSAY

David C. Larsen

Dr. David Larsen, Vice President
and Director of the Center for
Education Abroad (1988–).
(Photo by David Bennett;
Arcadia University Archives)

During the summer of 1948, Jack Wallace, a newly hired economics instructor, undertook a groundbreaking and significant venture. Professor Wallace and his wife took a class of 17 Beaver College students to Europe to study the economic effects of World War II and the post-war rebuilding efforts by looking at what was then happening in a number of cities in England and on the Continent. The group sailed across the Atlantic from New York to Southampton, traveled around England on used bicycles purchased there for this purpose, took the boat across the Channel, and continued riding their bikes through Belgium and France—all the way to Paris. They spent a total of eight weeks living and learning abroad before sailing back to New York at the end of the summer. Classes were taught on shipboard en route and in locales like Oxford, London and Paris during the program.

This was a pioneering and bold effort. In June of 1948, few other American colleges or universities had resurrected the study abroad programs that the World War had interrupted. Just two schools had been able to generate interest in overseas study, secure the necessary permissions, and make overseas arrangements capable of supporting the resumption of such undertakings. Only Beaver College was able to launch a new one. Professor Wallace developed his idea into an actual program during an era when international communications relied upon the postal services, when neither the telegraph nor the telephone was used for anything short of a true emergency. It was a time before easy and efficient transatlantic air travel, even before the advent of "student ships" that would encourage and support subsequent summer and semester-long study abroad programs throughout the 1950s and early 1960s.

The Beaver College students in Jack Wallace's class not only worked hard, they played hard—and they enjoyed themselves immensely. Contemporary campus folklore perpetuates descriptions of Beaver College women slogging through the rain on their heavy bikes, of late-night study sessions, of dances and parties with their English student counterparts (and even some local servicemen). Living conditions were just as "quaint" and primitive as the $2.00/day budgeted to pay for them would suggest. Remarkably, everyone coped cheerfully and the venture succeeded beyond the College's expectations.

This undertaking was such a hit that it was repeated in expanded format during the summers of 1949 and 1950. The itinerary broadened to include more of France and to add other European destinations. Bicycles were abandoned in favor of passage on the rebuilt European railway system. Under Professor and Mrs. Wallace's leadership, student participation grew each year. This summer program became so popular that when, after three years, Jack Wallace left Beaver College to teach at Boston University, other faculty members eagerly came forward to take up the reigns and to lead the project forward.

John Hathaway was one of these. A professor of fine arts, he arranged to add gallery visits in Spain and Italy to a busy itinerary of stops at sights in Belgium, Holland, France,

and Switzerland. The original academic focus, economic reconstruction, was replaced by a deliberate effort to see, discuss and understand European art. The number of participants increased. The thrill and excitement of education abroad continued. For nearly a decade following the first summer program in 1948, Beaver College undergraduates looked forward to the summer in Europe, now an attractive feature of the institution's curricular and co-curricular program and a special experience to which their enrollment at the Jenkintown/Glenside-based institution entitled them. In Arcadia's sesquicentennial year, alumnae and former faculty fondly and enthusiastically still recall their first-hand education on location in Europe—and all the surrounding activities and adventures—as being among the highlights of their lives.

Although the reasons for ending this annual summer practice in the late 1950s are obscure, Beaver College did suspend operation of this early post-war education abroad program at that time. But not for very long.

The students and Dr. Wallace with their RAF surplus bicycles on the dock in Belgium ready to head for Paris. On some days they biked as much as 60 miles. (Photo courtesy of Phyllis J. Weiner '51; Arcadia University Archives)

The entrance to the City
of London College in 1969.
(Arcadia University Archives)

When David Gray joined the Beaver College faculty in 1964, he brought more than an advanced degree in political science to Glenside. He had contacts and connections in London, an entrepreneurial vision, and the ability to convince others to let him give his creative ideas a try. Dr. Gray saw broad acceptance in American higher education of the "junior year abroad" experiences for language majors. Spending one's junior year immersed in on-site language study in France, Spain, Germany, or Italy was generally regarded as an effective learning experience by American colleges and universities during the decades between the World Wars of the 20th century. In the 1950s, it was rediscovered and reinvigorated. Participation was greater than ever by the early 1960s. At the same time, summer study and travel abroad experiences like the one Beaver College had pioneered were being developed for students in other academic fields. David Gray was determined to develop a third option—education abroad during the regular academic year for non-foreign language majors. He secured the College's approval, and on September 9, 1965, 24 Beaver College women, accompanied by Dr. and Mrs. Gray, disembarked at Southampton from the student ship "Aurelia." A new era of international education had begun.

After a few days sightseeing in the Salisbury/Stonehenge area, the Beaver College group arrived in London on September 19th. They were accommodated at the German Youth Hostel in Paddington. After London orientation and some special seminars on such subjects as the British systems of government and education, they attended regular fall term classes at City of London College.

Harry Beecheno, a City of London College department head, facilitated the Beaver College group's integration into academic life there. In addition, the group participated in visits to places of interest in and around London. They shared lodgings, showers and kitchens at the youth hostel, which led, sometimes, to the brink of creative disaster and to no end of amusement. It was an extraordinarily rich semester of both classroom-based and experiential learning.

The academic program ended with mid-December exams. Then the students went off for a weeklong Christmas-time "homestay" with British families, followed by two weeks of visits to several European capital cities before returning to the United States around the middle of January. Full credit for work done in England was readily accepted by Beaver College for each participant, and an institution was born—the Beaver College Center for Education Abroad.

David Gray's experimental program directly addressed an unmet educational need among American undergraduates. Students welcomed a way to enroll overseas in an English-speaking country—indeed, in England itself—for academic credit that would transfer back and be counted toward degree requirements at their home schools. Creation of the College Center for Education Abroad at Beaver provided a mechanism for doing exactly that. All students enrolled in the London Semester program received a Beaver College transcript—documentation from an accredited American institution of the courses taken, their credit value, and the grades earned in recognizable American terms. Registrars and credit transfer officers on home campuses no longer had to puzzle over unfamiliar documents of foreign origin. Credit for study in London now could be understood and transferred in as readily as could credit from any other American institution.

David Gray recognized two other things during that first year: there was unfilled capacity at British universities to absorb bright American students; and there were a large number of non-language majors on U.S. campuses who wanted to enroll for a year or a semester abroad. CCEA would bring these two elements together.

The early staff of the College Center for Education Abroad included Dr. Gray as director, assisted by Marjorie (Marj) Holler and by Carolyn Watson (one of the student participants in the 1965 Beaver group). Harry Beecheno worked in many capacities in London —he recruited faculty to teach, helped with orientation and arrival services, and handled advising and trouble-shooting. He did this part-time until his retirement from City of London College in 1975, and then full-time for several more years. During the first decade of this program, Beaver College faculty members were recruited to spend a year in London as resident directors and sometimes as instructors for the program.

At home, the College Center for Education Abroad (CCEA) reached out to other institutions in the mid-Atlantic and New England regions. A consortium was formed with Beaver College, Franklin and Marshall College, and Yale University. Managed by Dr. Gray, the College Consortium for Education Abroad actively recruited American undergraduate students (almost always juniors) at first to the London Semester program and then also to full-year, direct enrollment at such other British universities as the University of Bangor in Wales, the University of Lancaster, the University of Surrey and some of the colleges of the University of London.

As enrollments grew rapidly and new program sites were added during those early years, CCEA organized advisory boards. At first, these were separate bodies in the United States and in Britain, but they later were united into a single body of study abroad advisors (from the few campuses where those officers existed), deans and academic advisors, Junior Year Abroad administrators, and, occasionally, registrars from both the United States and Britain. Participants used the bi-annual meetings of this group for the purposes of sharing information, suggesting new programs, establishing policy, discussing student recruitment, and reviewing and re-confirming the validity of Beaver's credit and grade translation practices.

By the early 1970s, CCEA offered study abroad opportunities in Britain, Vienna and Hong Kong. Mrs. Holler was managing publicity and the administration, and coordinating responsibilities for the Glenside staff. Carolyn Watson spent part of her time each year visiting American campuses and talking with prospective students and advisors. David Gray handled relations with the consortium and overseas partners. He also directed the business aspects of the operation, establishing a solid operating base.

The dissolution of the Beaver-led consortium a few years later (when Yale decided to go its own way with a program in Hong Kong and Franklin and Marshall lost interest) did not significantly disrupt operations. Enrollments steadily increased as the Beaver College Center for Education Abroad carried on these overseas programs alone. Beaver had established a year-round program in Vienna, Austria, led by Professor Chris Latour, and developed more university-based sites in the United Kingdom to provide further options for students who sought a more fully integrated experience than the London Semester provided. It began a relationship with Trinity College in Dublin, opening Ireland as an additional Junior Year Abroad destination for American undergraduates.

Faculty member Helene Cohan was seconded from the Foreign Language Department to assist CCEA with the management of the Vienna Semester program. Later, responsibility for programs in Ireland was added to her administrative mandate. She successfully administered programs in both those countries (and in Greece in the 1990s) for several years.

By the time Tom Roberts joined the staff in 1979, Beaver's programs were ready for rapid domestic expansion. An experienced student recruiter for study abroad, Mr. Roberts quickly succeeded in broadening the recruiting base from a focus on the eastern third of the United States to include the whole country. Thus Beaver College's study abroad program, already one of America's oldest, became one of its largest. The following decade saw enrollments grow dramatically.

In the early 1980s, new British program sites were developed both in and out of London. The London School of Economics signed on with both full-year and special single-term options. Irish universities in Cork and Galway also joined the Beaver list. Affiliation with the Austro-American Institute for Education strengthened the Vienna Semester program. The popularity of London as a study abroad destination generated a constant need for student accommodations there. That combined with the need for a "permanent" Beaver College base in Europe to justify the College's taking a long-term lease on Shield House in London's South Kensington neighborhood.

In addition to generating a financial surplus which provided vital revenue for Beaver College's annual operations, the programs provided by the College Center for Education Abroad helped the College gain national and international recognition. While this was happening, however, the number of Beaver College undergraduates participating in its study abroad program gradually declined. As enrollments on the Glenside campus shrank during the 1980s, students were discouraged from going abroad, since their absence from campus meant lost residence hall revenue. In the 1986–87 academic year, there were no students from Beaver College among the 1,500 who studied overseas through CCEA.

David Gray and Tom Roberts left Beaver College in 1988. The new director of the Center for Education Abroad, David Larsen, faced a formidable task. Not only did he need to carry forward a highly successful operation, but he also faced a new and extraordinary competitive challenge: David Gray and Tom Roberts soon returned to international education as the leaders of a new study abroad institute based at Butler University in Indiana.

Dr. David Gray, Assistant Professor of Political Science, Vice President and Director of the Beaver College Center for Education Abroad (1964–1988). (Arcadia University Archives)

Students arrive at Shield House in 1986, one of the first Beaver College residences in London. The building also housed Beaver College's London office. It enjoyed a splendid location in South Kensington on Egerton Gardens near the Victoria and Albert Museum. (Arcadia University Archives)

Two CEA students in front of the Tower Bridge, London, England. (Photo by Lionel Delevingne, Leeds, Ma.; Arcadia University Archives)

CEA students in the harbor of Sydney, Australia, with the Opera House in the background. (Photo by Lionel Delevingne, Leeds, Ma.; Arcadia University Archives)

Dr. Larsen decided that the Beaver College program needed to change. During the next decade, he worked with the staff to strengthen existing programs and to add new institutions and new destinations to Beaver's already extensive list. Assisted by Peggy Stone, Arlene Snyder, Julia Levy, Christina Good and later by Lorna Stern on the Glenside campus, Dr. Larsen hired permanent, full-time resident directors abroad and recruited and developed a talented staff for the Glenside office and in the field. The role of the overseas offices was expanded from student services to include responsibility for program administration. As the number of study sites grew, year-round offices were established in Dublin, Edinburgh, Athens, Guadalajara, Melbourne, and Queenstown, New Zealand. Additionally, programs in Spain and Italy were added. Full-time resident directors were hired and trained to help assure optimum program quality: Will Migniuolo (Great Britain), Jan Motyka Sanders (Greece), Colin Ireland (Ireland), Ana Isabel Sousa (Mexico), Carmelle Le Vin (Australia), and Jane Gunn-Lewis (New Zealand).

A small team of regional representatives carries information and descriptive materials about the Arcadia University Center for Education Abroad (CEA) to campuses throughout the United States. These five assistant directors visit some 300 campuses each year to make presentations to students, faculty and advisors.

A group of 40 study-abroad professionals from around the country works closely with CEA staff as a National Advisory Board. They provide feedback and suggestions about ongoing activities and indicate program developments to meet the emerging interests and academic needs of undergraduates. Internships, summer programs, service learning opportunities and freshman year activities have been developed in response to the Board's suggestions.

CEA provides American undergraduates access to some seventy overseas programs in Australia, England, Greece, Ireland, Italy, Mexico, New Zealand, Scotland, Spain, and Wales. The Arcadia University Center for Education Abroad is a national leader—one of America's oldest and largest education abroad programs. CEA strives consistently to provide the highest level of support and service to its program participants wherever they are in the world.

Mr. Will Migniuolo, Deputy Director for CEA's British Operations, shares his vast knowledge of English History and London with students during the 1996 London Preview trip. (Arcadia University Archives)

London Preview students, Caitlin Dollarton '04, Stas Onishchenko '04, Jamie Townsend '04, and Esther Rineer '04, explore a phone booth in England during the March 2001 trip. (Photo courtesy of Stas Onishchenko '04, Philadelphia, Pa.; Arcadia University Archives)

For more than one-third of its 150-year history, Arcadia University has been actively involved in international education. In 2001–02, more than 2,000 American students from more than 350 home colleges and universities studied abroad as participants in one or more of Arcadia University's programs. Servicing a range of students, new high school graduates through master's degree candidates, in a variety of program structures (summer, a single semester, and full year), the Center for Education Abroad makes serious overseas learning experiences, and appropriately documented credit for them, available around the globe.

But that is not all. Throughout the 1990s and into the 21st century, this institution's Trustees, Administration, and Faculty have collaborated with CEA to find creative and effective ways to implement that component of the University's mission which involves "preparing students for life in a changing global society." Arcadia University has steadily become an institution where students can come to learn about—and to experience—the world. The curriculum changed to reflect an international perspective; new undergraduate and graduate programs with an international emphasis were developed. Increasingly, Arcadia University students were encouraged to study abroad and were supported by the University in their efforts to do so. Short-term, faculty-designed and -led Arcadia University programs took students to destinations around the world during vacation periods; most academic programs provided a study abroad option allowing undergraduates to fulfill requirements for the major overseas without delaying the date of graduation. Some academic majors require a semester or more of overseas experience; the study of languages received renewed emphasis and support, and Arcadia's unique "London Preview" used CEA's overseas resources and structures to allow every freshman the chance to spend spring break in London for a nominal fee.

Arcadia University was being transformed into a truly internationalized institution, with flags from CEA affiliate countries adorning campus walkways, and faculty competing for financial support for travel and research abroad. Students reported having decided to come to Arcadia because of its international involvement and the opportunities it provides for them. About 70% of the freshmen participated in London Preview each year. Most of the faculty and a large percentage of the staff who wish to accompany them have done so. In 2001–02, more than 100 Arcadia undergraduates studied abroad for credit—a clear indication of the progress this University has made during the past fifteen years.

The curricular and programmatic initiatives developed together by CEA and Arcadia University's faculty and administrators led, in 2001, to this institution's recognition by the American Council on Education as one of only eight colleges and universities in the country whose efforts at institution-wide internationalization constitute "promising practices" for others to follow in the future.

The Center for Education Abroad's Glenside offices at 1601 Church Road. The building was initially built to provide power for the trolley that ran from Glenside to Willow Grove Park. (Photo by Bill Avington, University Relations, Arcadia University, Glenside, Pa.; Arcadia University Archives)

A VISION FOR THE FUTURE OF ARCADIA UNIVERSITY

PART V

Bette E. Landman

Time present and time past

Are both perhaps present in time future,

And time future contained in time past.[18]

This fragment from T. S. Eliot's poem *Burnt Norton* captures so much about Arcadia University today. Our successes and our future plans continue to grow seamlessly out of our 150-year history. We honor that proud past as we shape, with integrity, a bold educational institution of the future.

| [18] Eliot, T.S. (1943). *Four quartets.* New York: Brace and Company (page 13).

Arcadia University students on the parapets of Grey Towers Castle.
(Photo by Todd A. Trice, Fairless Hills, Pa.; Arcadia University Archives)

A VISION FOR THE FUTURE OF ARCADIA UNIVERSITY

At the time that this book is being written, the campus is in the throes of planning for its

next ten years. When I look at some of the initiatives that are already underway and add

these to my own dreams and to the emerging goals growing out of the planning process,

I believe I can see some key features of the first decades of the next fifty years, the time

leading up to our bicentennial.

PRESERVING THE BEST OF THE PAST

As this sesquicentennial volume amply illustrates, our institution has had an enviable record of being at the cutting edge of responsible and pioneering change. Two centuries ago, we were one of the nation's first women's colleges. We continued to lead the way in the 1950s and 1960s by opening our doors to mature women who wished to pursue degrees on a part-time basis. In the 1970s, we were among the earliest non-historically Black colleges to champion educational access for persons of color. We also were one of a handful of institutions that pioneered study abroad for non-language majors; were one of the first small four-year colleges to introduce extensive graduate and evening programs to serve working adults; were one of three higher education institutions nationwide that gave birth to the concept of writing-across-the-curriculum; and were in the vanguard of

a movement to enhance the teaching of critical thinking, problem solving, and collaborative learning. In addition, many of our alumni will recall doing volunteer work in the schools and at social agencies fully three decades before the current service learning movement. Most recently, as noted in the essay in this book on the Center for Education Abroad, Arcadia was again singled out for its educational leadership when it was named by the American Council on Education and the Carnegie Corporation as one of just eight colleges and universities in the United States possessing the best "promising practices" for internationalizing its curriculum.

Now, with our new name and status, we once again dedicate ourselves to remaining true to the central themes which make this a special place. We reaffirm those characteristics that have defined and differentiated our institution from its beginning: quality education,

174

The Institution's new name and status as displayed on a 2001 pennant. (Photo by Jerome Lukowicz, Philadelphia, Pa.; Arcadia University Archives)

personal attention, a dedicated faculty and staff, and a commitment to providing educational access to all. We believe, as we always have, that students learn best in the face-to-face intimate atmosphere of small classes taught by fully qualified, caring faculty who are attentive to the needs and potential of each student. Our challenge, as we look to the future, is to determine how we can best use the capacity of the University and the tools of the modern age to ensure preservation of these essential values and commitments, while anticipating the kinds of skills and understandings that students will need in an increasingly complex and interdependent global society.

WHAT THE NEW UNIVERSITY MAY BECOME

What does it mean to be a university, and what changes might occur? We are likely to become a larger institution, not large like the major state universities, but larger than the 3,000 students on our campus at the sesquicentennial. We can see reasons to add a few hundred more undergraduates in order to continue building on what we learned in the 1990s: educational quality and the quality of campus life can only continue to flourish if we are self-sufficient, and we can only be self-sufficient with a healthy enrollment. A larger student body will, by its nature, be more differentiated, offering the promise of sustaining a greater breadth of academic majors, depth on athletic teams, and range of club and social activities. Such growth, though, will require several major new

commitments—residence hall construction, additional support staff, and, most importantly, additional faculty to ensure that our traditions and values are maintained.

As we grow, we will strive to reach one of our long-standing goals, a greater degree of gender balance among our undergraduates. We will remain committed, more than ever, to having a campus that is fully reflective of the diversity of backgrounds in our nation; there is no other way to provide a realistic education for our students. With greater numbers, we can continue the progress we have already made in selectivity and in entering credentials (SATs, ACTs, class rank, etc.). We will return to having a wider geographic representation among our students, and have greater numbers of international students studying with us, either full-time or in exchange relationships.

Graduate programs will almost certainly multiply. There will be an ever-growing demand for post-graduate education, shaped largely by the needs of the workplace. Some of this will call forth new degree programs, while much may take the form of certificate or continuing education programs. It is not likely, however, that new graduate programs will include Ph.D. studies, for they require a commitment in faculty time and institutional resources that exceed our current or short-term future capacity. Other professional doctorates, however, modeled on our D.P.T. and Ed.D., but in entirely new disciplines and professional fields, might well be on the horizon. Some programs may be held at off-campus locations. Some

Arcadia University mathematics students with their counterparts at East China Normal University (ECNU), in Shanghai, May 2002. From left to right, Agnes Yeboah '03, Jessica Jubok '02, Tom Newman (partly obscured) '02, Patti DeBow '02, Amon Wilkes '02 (profile, partly obscured). ECNU students not identified. (Photo by Steven Goldberg, Arcadia University, Glenside, Pa.; Arcadia University Archives)

might be partly or largely taught remotely, via the Internet or whatever communication technology supercedes it.

THE CORE OF MY DREAM FOR OUR FUTURE

If all the above comes to pass, Arcadia University will be the kind of community it has always been, albeit different in scale. It will continue to be a special place to its alumni, and a special place to work. But what will make us special, noteworthy, even outstanding? Happily, we are poised to build upon our strengths in a way that assures our uniqueness and also meets the emerging needs of our nation.

The next ten years will see Arcadia University amplifying the leadership it has already demonstrated in international education. That leadership rests on the successes of our Center for Education Abroad and the creativity of our faculty. We have developed such features as an innovative core curriculum; the London Preview program; so-called "sandwich courses" which take students abroad in the middle of a course; new majors and minors in such areas as international studies, business and culture, international peace and conflict resolution; overseas biodiversity preservation projects; and opportunities for service learning, student teaching, internships, and clinical rotations abroad. Faculty are taking advantage of the Center for Education Abroad's ties to more than 70 universities in 13 countries to enrich on-campus teaching and learning in partnerships with colleagues and disciplinary peers around the world.

Electronic communication can bring these international resources right into Glenside classrooms. For example, through interactive video, students in any major can enjoy a presentation, ask questions, and engage in dialogue with noted faculty, artists, business and political figures from other universities and countries. Our faculty in Greece could offer a course where students on our campus are treated to real-time tours of archaeological sites and historic structures in Delphi, Ephesus, or Athens, or even a city in ancient Arcadia. Arcadia faculty could work with international teaching partners to develop courses that share the same syllabus and set of research topics. Such an effort has begun. By means of e-mail, the Web, and the Internet, our students are already paired with student research partners abroad to write a paper collaboratively or engage in learning exercises that profit from input from diverse cultures and different points of view. In the spring of 2002, a combined undergraduate and graduate class spent two weeks at the end of the semester in China completing their work with "classmates" at East China Normal University in Shanghai.

I believe that we will use our extensive international contacts to expand language learning. Although 56% of our faculty report having second language ability, most have had little chance to keep their skills well honed. I foresee significant numbers of faculty spending a sabbatical semester or shorter periods abroad both polishing language mastery and setting up

Associate Professor and Co-Chair of the Department of Political Science Joan Hulse Thompson (1986–) consults with Kevin Sangster '99. (Photo by Peter Finger, Glenmont, N.Y.; Arcadia University Archives)

international courses that Arcadia students in all disciplines can take, perhaps even a "language-across-the-curriculum" program. International faculty counterparts would also be spending weeks or semesters teaching on the Glenside campus. In these ways, our students, even if they study only in Glenside, have exposure to a varied and specialized, world-renowned faculty—a feature typically found only in large research universities, and even then, usually limited to graduate students. Unlike large university settings, however, our students will be experiencing these contacts in small, personal classes where faculty are directly guiding the learning process.

Students planning to participate in study abroad or in classes on campus that are paired with international research partners will take "survival language courses" to help them understand the subtleties of the culture and learn the basic language skills needed to interact in the other country. In this way, language learning becomes an organic part of curriculum and students' interest. Arcadia's international ties, its location in a rich local higher education environment, and the presence of the American Language Academy on campus mean that through faculty exchange, international student language partners, and distance learning, our students can elect to study almost any language in the world.

Such international collaboration will provide the basis for offering multi-disciplinary area study programs as major courses of study and as minors that can supplement any program. I can envision a confluence of academic strengths on campus and through our Center for Education Abroad leading to an International Studies major, perhaps centered on the Mediterranean. Arcadia faculty partnerships in China, Korea, and Australia may provide the nucleus for an Asian Studies concentration on our campus. I anticipate other area studies programs to emerge by similar means.

As our faculty become experts in the many facets of cross-cultural understanding, they will possess the potential to provide special services to the industries and corporations in our region. As more businesses enter the international marketplace, and as experienced companies seek to expand their global reach, I believe that we would be in a good position to provide cultural and language training to help make these corporate initiatives more successful. These efforts would build on the fine masters degree program we already offer in International Peace and Conflict Resolution, as well as provide a basis for master's level work in international business and culture. Ultimately, I see all of these innovations being drawn together in an Arcadia University International Studies Center, where corporate, government, diplomatic, and educational institutions would look to us for high quality preparation in careers that cross national boundaries.

Surely another component of our near future will be the fuller integration of electronic technology into the learning process at this University. It may seem paradoxical, but we are learning that technology, if used properly, can actually enhance the personal nature of education. Faculty can use computers to engage students more completely in classroom participatory exercises, out-of-class discussions via chat rooms, interaction with faculty and fellow students as readers for works in process, and as a tool to extend the classroom experience for students who wish to explore further the topics that interest them. We anticipate using these tools to allow classroom and faculty/student contact time to be used more intensively as a forum for information analysis and in-depth understanding. To that end, Arcadia has constructed Brubaker Hall as a technologically sophisticated learning center. The beginning of our sesquicentennial year will coincide with the opening of the new library, which will contain state-of-the-art wireless access to information technology.

I suspect that soon, students—using either their laptops, or, more likely in a few years, hand-held devices—will be able to access almost all of the information that now takes them to such places as the business office to check on the balance of their accounts, to the registrar to see their transcripts or the status of their registration for the coming semester, or to the dining hall to learn of the current week's activities schedule. At Arcadia, information technology will be a tool to enhance student access to one another, to faculty, and to the institution.

As much as I hope our students feel that they are citizens of the world, I know that most will spend their lives largely in the United States. For that simple reason, we have no choice but to create an institution that brings together all the peoples of this land.

Our University, from its founding, has been an institution committed to access and diversity. We, perhaps alone among America's higher education institutions, now have an opportunity to use innovations that we have developed in the study of other countries to extend our students' understanding and appreciation of the rich diversity of our own society. Our current team-taught, multidisciplinary general education core courses provide the underpinnings for such an initiative. "Justice: Multicultural Perspectives," required of first-year students, analyzes issues of social justice in all times and places; the second, "Pluralism in the United States," required of sophomores, focuses on understanding the rich variety of different peoples, religions, classes, age groups, etc. that comprise the citizenry of the United States.

By the year 2020, if current birth rates and patterns of immigration continue, the minority populations of 20th-century America will collectively constitute the majority of the 21st. Whether students become teachers, artists, doctors, physical therapists, or leaders in world-wide commerce and industry, they will increasingly find themselves working in settings where cultures, languages, attitudes, and values will be different from their own. How can we ensure that our graduates can productively negotiate and appreciate this rich heritage? We can use our international studies model to good effect in our own country. Why not provide students with a sophomore spring break "preview" experience that exposes them to one or more of the diverse cultural settings in North and Central America—Puerto Rico, a tribal reservation, Appalachia, Quebec, etc? These experiences could stand alone or include civic and social service opportunities. Just as we broker student and faculty exchanges with higher education institutions abroad, why not provide exchanges with historically Black colleges and universities (HBCUs), predominantly Hispanic or tribal institutions? Can we not also have professors from these schools as "guest" lecturers via interactive video, as research partners with our faculty, or as exchange professors? Can not our faculty arrange "sandwich" courses that take the students to areas of the United States over the inter-semester break, or develop collaborative syllabi with other faculty that pair our students with those at a culturally different American institution?

IN CONCLUSION, A BEGINNING

Whether our time horizon is the next 150 years, or the next 50, or 10, or next year, how well can we predict the future? Surely, predictive power decreases over time. The future, however, is partly in our own hands. In the years since 1985, we have learned to plan. We have learned that we can be proactive in our choices of educational futures, that, within limits, we can determine what we wish to be as an institution and we can take the steps to bring that vision about. This represents both an important change in attitude and a change in institutional capacity; we have come to believe that we can plan and see results, and we have the means to do so.

I do not contend that we can transcend the cycles of the economy, the vagaries of politics, or the forces of nature. There will be reversals, even mistakes, as Arcadia University goes forward. There will be new and consequential developments that we can not now imagine. Remember that only 25 years ago there were no personal computers, no Internet, no cell phones. The key to institutional prosperity and constant educational progress is awareness. We must, and I am sure we will, continue to plan with full understanding of the broader environment in which we operate. That includes knowing where we have been, which we now understand far better because of the research done in the preparation of this book.

Whatever elements of my vision come to reality, and I am certain some will, the threads of quality and caring that reach back 150 years will weave through the new institutional fabric. Arcadia University embodies Beaver College, and both live in the minds of alumni past and future. With the beneficence of its sons and daughters, the vitality of its faculty and staff, and the curiosity of its students, Arcadia will continue as a beacon of learning and personal growth for decades to come.

A remarkable journey, a limitless future. (Photo by Jon D. Adams, Hi5 Photos, Jenkintown, Pa.; Arcadia University Archives)